Can These Dry Bones Live?

Can These Dry Bones Live?

An Introduction to Christian Theology

FRANCES YOUNG

The Pilgrim Press
Cleveland, Ohio

Originally published by SCM Press, Ltd., London,
as *Can These Dry Bones Live? The Excitement of
Theological Study,* © 1982, 1992
by Frances M. Young

Pilgrim Press edition published 1993
The Pilgrim Press, Cleveland, Ohio 44115

Printed in the United States of America

The paper used in this publication is acid free and
meets the minimum requirements of American
National Standard for Information
Sciences-Permanence of Paper for Printed Library
Materials, ANSI Z39.48-1984

98   97   96   95   94   93   5   4   3   2   1

Library of Congress Cataloging-in-Publication Data

Young, Frances M. (Frances Margaret)
Can these dry bones live? : an introduction to
Christian theology / Frances Young.
p.   cm.
Includes bibliographical references and index.
ISBN 0-8298-0968-6 (alk. paper)
1. Theology.   I. Title.
BR118.Y69   1993
230—dc20   93-8226
                                               CIP

In memory of my brother Richard,
who had he lived would have been a student
of theology and a minister of the church,
and whose loss first taught me of
God's absence and God's presence.

CONTENTS

PREFACE

The years pass, and the pilgrimage goes on. Yet some insights never date – to change the metaphor, they become building-blocks for new structures. And some issues never go away – they are simply too pivotal. All of this is true of this little book, first written as a Lent book for 1982, but still important to me and, it seems, valued and requested by others.

Two *insights* have grown in importance. One is the intriguing use of music as a parable. When later I realized that the debate concerning 'authentic performance' provided genuine parallels to questions raised by new approaches to biblical interpretation, I found I was not the first to explore the possibilities. However, as the analogy developed I was amazed at the expanding fruitfulness of its cultivation. It became the organizing theme of my *Virtuoso Theology: The Bible and Interpretation* (The Pilgrim Press, 1993).

The other is the image of the woman in travail. As feminist theology has provoked reservations and enthusiasm, the importance of biblical material which uses female analogies for divine activity has grown. So too has the importance of a theology of creation and new creation, a theme so intimately related in this study with the mother in labour, and now so relevant to the new bandwagon of 'green theology'. Too often the creation theme is divorced from the themes of salvation and atonement, but in the Christian tradition they are inseparable and complementary. A reminder of that remains timely. Meanwhile, however, my own explorations have led me in the unexpected direction of the Virgin Mary. Neglected by Protestants and problematic for Catholic women, for them representing as she does the impossible ideal of virgin and mother and confining them in the eyes of their church to those roles and those alone, I begin to believe that she is a potent symbol of the travailing creation, and of the suffering and redemption of the church. My meditations have yet to be fully developed, but meanwhile I have become a Patron of the Ecumenical Society of the Blessed Virgin Mary.

Two *issues* were married, perhaps not altogether happily, in this little book, and both of those remain alive. True the doctrine of atonement is not currently among the fashionable trends of theology. Theology and church life has been deeply affected in the last ten – twenty years by secular movements world-wide, so that the talking points have been liberation, peace, multiculturalism, ecology and sexuality, and the signs are that in the 1990s wealth creation, the market economy, science and technology are beginning to join them. It is, of course, important that theology is engaged with the contemporary world, and that is not the least of the pleas made here – we cannot simply repeat the dogmas of the past without re-thinking in relation to present culture. But there is another sense in which the world should not be allowed to set the whole agenda of Christian theology. Christianity makes claims about how the world is, and these claims may dramatically affect the perspective within which the world's agenda is dealt with. Not only has the evangelical tradition placed atonement at the heart of the Christian gospel, but suffering, sin and salvation are inevitably recurring themes in any theology which addresses the world as it is. In the end discussion of those subjects in a Christian context cannot steer entirely clear of the traditional language and imagery of the cross and the atoning sacrifice of Christ. That being the case, we have to continue to address the perennial questions concerning how that act of God can be appropriated as meaningful and understood as effective.

The other issue, with which the book opens, is the place of

academic and critical theology in the life of the Christian disciple. Tension and misunderstanding continues unabated between academics on the one hand, and on the other, so-called 'ordinary people' and the churches. Theological students still find themselves faced with an academic diet concerning which they feel grave reservations, often because they prejudge it to be dangerous, irrelevant or plain boring. In many quarters the 'dry bones' of arid tomes are still awaiting the prophecy which might bring them to life. Yet the longer I live the less I can see the stereotype academic in the majority of my colleagues. If only that stereotype could be laid to rest! If only we could discover that all of us, at different levels, are pursuing the same quest, and that mutual respect and assistance might be creative! In so far as this book is an apology for academic theology, it surely still has important things to say.

When I wrote this apology, I and my church were coming to terms with my 'Damascus Road' call to ministry. On both sides adjustments were required to find the appropriate expression of a vocation to bridge the academy and the church. It has been a moving experience to find myself accepted and affirmed by the Methodist family. But from comments like, 'You're not like other theologians!' or expressions of surprise that people could understand the preaching of someone who 'must be very learned', I know how deeply the barriers are still entrenched – indeed reinforced by the acquisition of the title 'Professor'. If this book can continue to help people, perhaps especially students in theological colleges, to recognize that academic questions are largely an extension of the innocent but profound questions of a child, I shall be grateful. For me there never can be any gulf between theology and spirituality, the intellectual quest and the pilgrimage of discipleship.

Readers will notice, as I did on re-reading the book, that the language is sometimes not as sensitive to inclusiveness and reference to those with learning disabilities as it would be now. I have changed some blatant examples, but more was not possible.

Introduction:
Can These Dry Bones Live?

A few months ago I was travelling on the local cross-city train. Opposite me in the carriage sat a man whose rather childish behaviour and naïve interest in the railway alerted me to the fact that he was quite possibly a person who had learning difficulties. Alongside me was a young black woman with a child in a push-chair. The child was asleep and she was deeply engrossed in reading a Bible. As the train got under way, the man opposite, to my great surprise, also pulled a Bible out of his bag and began to read. I sat there fascinated and humbled, reflecting that in the days of the Reformation and the Evangelical Revival, the equivalent sight would not have occasioned surprise – for then the common people discovered the Bible, they learned to read because that gave access to the Bible, they were sure that the Bible had the words of life. People, even church people, are not so sure now, are they? What's the betting that both these people belonged to what respectable church people would dismiss as sects?

Not long ago I discovered a poem by George Herbert called *The Window*. It is about preaching, of all things!

> Lord, how can man preach thy eternal word?
> He is a brittle crazie glasse:
> Yet in thy temple thou dost him afford
> This glorious and transcendent place,
> To be a window, through thy grace.

But when thou dost anneal in glasse thy storie,
   Making thy life to shine within
The holy preachers; then the light and glorie
   More reverend grows, and more doth win:
   Which else shows watrish, bleak and thin.

Doctrine and life, colours and light, in one
   When they combine and mingle, bring
A strong regard and aw: but speech alone
   Doth vanish like a flaring thing,
   And in the eare, not conscience ring.

The Word preached and lived was for Herbert something beautiful, powerful, and the preacher's task was something awesome. Yet now preaching and piety are regarded as outmoded, even within church circles.

This book arises out of sadness and, I must confess, some degree of anger. I recall the minister's wife who, on learning what I intended to study at university, said, 'What on earth do you want to do that for?' I recall someone's reported reaction to a piece of my writing – it was a painful reflection on the moral implications of keeping handicapped children alive by modern medical techniques: 'Why doesn't she get out and do something?' I think of the long string of ordinands who have come to say they were giving up Greek because they could not see its relevance to their future ministry. There is a mood abroad in society which elevates activity at the expense of thought and disciplined study, which devalues pure research in favour of applied, which turns the word 'academic' into a word of criticism, a synonym for 'irrelevant', 'impractical' or 'niggling'. People are prepared to accept slipshod thinking and superficial slogans, as long as some practical contribution is the outcome. And this mood has invaded the church. The emphasis is on effective service and practical action, on pastoral work and being available to people willy-nilly, on political campaigning and social engagement. Of course such things are important, but I cannot help feeling that if everyone stopped rushing around in little circles and began to think about the centre of it all, then the enriched life of the church would in itself ensure that it had greater impact. People seem to assume that it is boring, ineffective, irrelevant to invest time and effort in disciplined study of the Bible and the Christian past, that preaching must be 'with it' or it is dead, that theological thinking is destructive – a burden for the church rather than an asset – and all we need is simple faith. How can they be so short-sighted? For me the theological quest has been vital, study of the Bible and the tradition crucial, the search for meaning central; and my own conviction is that a rediscovery of what it means to study the Bible and think theologically is essential for healthy life in the church. So in the first chapter I try to indicate why it is so important – and overall what I would like to stimulate by this book is renewed interest in serious theological study, particularly among ordinands and clergy, but also among educated lay people. I hope to be able to convey something of the excitement of wrestling with what might seem outmoded and irrelevant ways of thinking, the excitement of discovering their potential to effect a profound shift in perspective, a transformation of life, attitudes, relationships, a genuine conversion, real liberation, new birth, resurrection. This makes all the difference to the spirit in which practical action is undertaken.

So the underlying thrust of the book is to do with studying our Christian heritage in such a way as to appropriate it in the present, with continuity and discontinuity, with the delicate balance between respect and criticism essential to the on-going renewal of the church's faith. Many assume that the Bible and the creeds, the traditional doctrines, preaching, are dry bones, the dull debris left by the past. Others try to preserve the skeleton unchanged – fossilized. To both sides I want to retort, 'Well, can't these dry bones live?' And I trust that they can, because the imparting of new life seems to me to be at the heart of the Christian gospel.

In fact the title of the book has a twofold intent. For in attempting to convey something of the excitement of theological study, as well as the demands and discipline it imposes, the central chapters provide a kind of specimen study focussing on the meaning of atonement, and tackling that problem has itself led into the

3

theme of new life, to the central Christian perception of a good creation corrupted but in process of rebirth. If this book helps to bring alive that theme, then perhaps there is hope for the Bible, for preaching, for theological study, for the enrichment of worship and the revival of the church itself.

The Lord said to me, 'Can these dry bones live?' I answered, 'O Lord God, thou knowest.' He said, 'Prophesy to these bones . . . Behold I will cause breath to enter you, and you shall live . . . and you shall know that I am the Lord.'

(Ezek. 37.3–6)

I

As Little Children

Amen I say to you, unless you turn around and become as little children, you will never enter the kingdom of heaven (Matt. 18.3).

This well-known text is one that is easily sentimentalized. People assume that becoming as little children means returning to a state of innocence, or accepting things on trust without any question; in other words, retaining a simple faith. Yet no parent or school-teacher has any illusions about the innocence of children. Nor can those who actually deal with children imagine any normal child who passively takes in everything with unquestioning acceptance. Children are selfish and aggressive little beasts, easily jealous and ever demanding, and their questions are interminable. Indeed, the qualities that children have which adults often lose are these: an insatiable curiosity, an infuriating persistence in asking why or how, energy and drive to explore and discover, a touching sense of wonder and a tremendous capacity for enjoyment. Children are never content to live on the past or settle for the present, but are always looking forward to the future. Without these qualities, they could not learn or advance to maturity – indeed failure to reach out and grab the world is a sign of mental handicap. The healthy child is creative, imaginative and curious.

Now excessive daring and curiosity is, of course, a positive

5

danger, and as children grow they have to be restrained – they have to learn what is safe, to learn to respect the tolerance limits of other people – and so on. So a wall of inhibitions begins to hem them in. But could it not be that the quality Jesus saw in children was the freedom to respond naturally, to feel and express wonder and love and joy, to gaze wide-eyed with open mouth, and then to rush in and explore, probe, take to pieces, find out for themselves, not accept hearsay or be over-impressed by convention? Staid grown-ups were worried about Jesus' credentials, reacted against novelty, appealed to the good old traditions of Moses and the elders. Children threw caution to the winds.

But if one aspect of growing up is to acquire inhibitions, another is to gain maturity through experience. That process comes about by making mistakes yet not giving up, by asking, learning, discovering, by making the inheritance of culture and skill, knowledge and faith, one's own. Often children's questions seem naïve and amusing, and yet equally often they are exactly those that exercise the minds of sophisticated theologians. I quote from *Children's Letters to God*:

> Instead of letting people die and having to make new ones, why don't you just keep the ones you got now? Jane.

> Dear God, Are you real? Some people don't believe it. If you are, you better do something quick. Harriet Ann.

> Dear God, Your book has a lot of zip to it. I like science fiction stories. You had very good ideas and I would like to know where you found them. Your reader Jimmy.

> Dear God, What are colds for? Rodd W.[1]

The business of asking questions is essential for advance in understanding. The biggest educational tragedy is when curiosity ebbs, interest sags, and parrot-learning, dogmatism, indifference or cynicism takes over. To be as a little child is to keep on asking questions, to refuse to accept inadequate answers, to learn to re-open questions as necessary, never to take anything for granted, in fact, to be determined to get to the bottom of any subject that catches one's interest. In the business of growing up, if you do not go forward, you go backward.

Some of the New Testament letter writers were well aware of that: look at the Epistle to the Hebrews. The writer is addressing people who have lost the first excitement of their faith. They are beginning to compromise: once they were prepared to stand the heat – social ostracism, attacks on person and property, abuse – but now they are beginning to grow cool, to stay away from Christian meetings, to avoid confrontation. They ought to be Christian teachers by now, but they need people to go over the simple preliminaries again. They need milk, not solid food, for they have remained infants in the faith. Yet solid food is what they are given in this epistle – tough doctrine and scripture study because just staying with the elementary doctrines will not solve anything. Only progress to maturity will counteract their tendency to drop out. If you do not move forward, you move backward.

People with an enthusiasm invariably devote time and energy to studying it. Why are there so many magazines on gardening, model-making, electronics, computing, cooking, travel? Because people who are keen on doing something, know they can do better by reading about it, getting tips from other people, putting some time and effort into thinking about it. A cricket fan who can tell you the top scores or batting averages for any year this century can do so only because he has been so gripped by the subject that studying the statistics is a pleasure and memorizing them effortless. Most people are capable of such feats if they are really committed to something. In my experience as a teacher of the subject, commitment to learning New Testament Greek contributes far more to eventual success than innate ability. But how many are prepared to put that kind of time and effort into studying and thinking about their Christian faith and its fundamental basis in the Bible and the creeds? How many want to go on to maturity? How many are prepared to examine things for themselves and think things through rather than just accepting them on trust? Of course there is a fundamental simplicity about the faith which can be grasped by the youngest child and the least intelligent. But there is also a richness and a complexity, a depth which demands effort; and it is a scandal that for so many their faith has not even the status of a hobby. When people are asked to study their faith before preaching, or to attain certain qualifications before ordination, it is not because the church has adopted false academic values from the rest of society; it is because attention to study is a measure of how serious people really are about their commitment. If you do not go forward, you go backward. Besides, we do not value very much something that has cost us nothing in time, effort or expense.

All too often people regard theology as an academic discipline remote from the world and from prayer, an intellectual ivory tower for which disengagement and objectivity are the cultivated attitudes. Yet, between theology and faith, theology and life, there is an intimate relationship. For the questions posed by everyday existence are profoundly theological ones, and prayer of any depth requires theological content and theological reflection. The Fathers of the church would be very puzzled to realize the dichotomies between the church and theology which now appear to exist. There is a need for the church to appropriate its theological heritage, and that involves academic study. There is a need for integration, for the recognition that a person's intellect plays its part in his experience as much as his feelings and actions, that critical theology has a role in the response of faith and the expression of commitment. There is a need for integrating critical and confessional use of the Bible, for the theologian and the preacher to find a common identity. The word 'critical' in this context refers to a process of *investigation*, asking questions, and that process is by no means a purely negative one. It can be constructive, liberating and exciting. Yet generations of ordinands are introduced to academic theology and then fail to communicate it, abandoning the task of relating it to their ministry in the parochial setting. Then periodically a work of critical theology bursts into public view, and largely because of that failure of communication, it produces scandal among the faithful. This failure is the sad outcome of the tensions and strains experienced by clergy who dare not openly utilize their critical

8

theology in their preaching; sometimes one fears they have even suppressed it in their thinking. They believe, I think mistakenly, that ordinary people do not ask questions; they fail to realize that in their own way, many are making decisions about theological issues in an unsophisticated and commonsense manner – some staying with the church but with reservations, many others abandoning ship. Often, sad to say, this withdrawal is the result of a naïve grasp of the faith – sheer ignorance of what the more sophisticated theological stance of the tradition actually has been and is.

That ordinary people do ask questions is proved by the case of a life-long lay Christian, who retired a couple of years ago, and to occupy himself during the idle winter months, began to write. He is an 'ordinary man' – left school at fourteen, had no educational advantages, worked hard all his life at very ordinary jobs. Yet he knows that theological questions are unavoidable. He cares about integrity and honesty. He worries that the church is weak and obscurantist, desperately demanding that people believe six incredible things before breakfast. Here are extracts from what he wrote:

> It is unfortunate but nevertheless a fact that the Christian church as a whole is losing ground so far as active membership is concerned, simply because on conscience grounds they cannot any longer keep up a charade. I know from personal experience how difficult it is to support certain dogmas to-day . . .

> As a non-conformist I have never felt any constraint in the pursuit of truth. However, it has often been a painful experience to meet people outside the church who are so sincere that they simply cannot enter into corporate worship because they cannot repeat a creed without a feeling of hypocrisy . . .

> From my conversations over the years, I am persuaded that a large proportion, unlettered as well as lettered, earnestly want the truth. In these less primitive days, i.e. as far as worldly knowledge is concerned, many long for the truth and are not afraid of an honest answer . . . to many, however, the

church appears to be talking to modern maturity as though it were a baby in arms . . .

The easiest way to be disliked and sometimes even disowned, is to fall out of line with the mainstream. Now I am not for one moment suggesting that the non-conformist churches disown their members who cannot go all the way with their affirmation of faith; on the contrary, one is very conscious of their concern and willingness to respect one's beliefs if sincerely held. Nevertheless a barrier is created, not by the minister or the congregation; it is the very fact that it is a sheer impossibility for the one who doubts, questions or even disbelieves certain dogmatic statements of faith to leave a service spiritually uplifted if one has not been able to participate to the full . . .

Despite our advance in understanding past history through agencies such as archaeology and improved perception of languages and their roots, the church appears hidebound and fearful of change. Surely no one seriously believes that the earth is flat or supports the seventeenth-century Bishop Ussher's calculations that the beginning of the world was at 9.0 a.m. on the 23rd October 4004 BC. A child of average intelligence knows better. If the church that has been built on the example of the life and teaching of Jesus is to survive into eternity, it must proclaim truth as an absolute as well as love. Truth and love are indivisible . . .

That there was a man called by the name Jesus, there is not any doubt. Certainly of a host of people that I have met both in and out of the churches, very few deny him as a truly historical person. I have met atheists who quite willingly recognize him as one of the world's greats, humanists applaud his revolutionary ideals . . . What many simply cannot accept is the supernaturalism attributed to his birth and the hidden years. The Sermon on the Mount cannot be faulted. What, then, was in the mind of this historical Jesus as he was endeavouring to teach, or shall I say lead, his contemporaries to a concept of God that was foreign to their traditional beliefs?

Did Jesus at the time of his baptism envisage that enormous edifices would be built ... to his eternal glory? to be worshipped as the only begotten Son of God? or was his only concern to walk humbly with God and carry the sacred flame into the world about him ...

[handwritten margin note: J, only concern]

Whilst man has undoubtedly progressed as science has become the central pivot of human understanding, it is natural that any form of supernaturalism has become open to question and questioning has long since ceased to be the prerogative of the academics. After thirty years as a sales representative in the medical field and nearly twenty years in industry, I have met many thoughtful personalities. The person on the shop floor can and does hold to some beliefs that would most certainly be anathema in my early years, and what is more they can give a good reasoned exposition ...

Anyone who spends his weekday evenings in hotels over the countryside finds that after several visits to a particular place he's almost certain to become on good conversational terms with his fellow-travellers. The fact that we are all so different in outlook often makes topical conversation so interesting. The same applies to the factory canteen where matters of moment continue from one lunch hour to the next. My own experiences convince me that a true atheist is very rare. I have often felt that doubters are unsure of the doubts they express. Today through the medium of wireless and television, people are being acquainted with a variety of subjects that otherwise would not have entered their minds. Travel, natural history, the evolution of man and his idea of God, comparative religion are subjects that are easily at hand in our libraries. What is more, they are being read, for the dates of issue to the readers testify to this. It seems that literacy is in the ascendant; fundamentalism is being challenged as never before. I do not feel that this is something to be feared but rather welcomed, for it indicates that a renewed search for truth is replacing dogmatic demands that have caused so much frustration which impedes rather than aids spiritual experience ... However,

[handwritten margin note: Question is Sad]

inasmuch as I believe that the creeds present no stumbling-block to many millions of Christians, I am nevertheless concerned for the multitude who remain outside the dynamic influence of the life of Jesus the transformer ... I have always held great admiration for the many non-committed persons who deprive themselves of Christian fellowship simply because they cannot in all honesty accept the supernaturalism of the creeds ... I know that so many people who are by no means anti-social are set apart by what I can only describe as intellectual honesty. Certainly churchgoers do not have a monopoly where integrity is concerned ... Jesus has captured the hearts of many more than our church records tell us. More are praying in the privacy of their homes than in churches. In my experience I have found many who say without the least embarrassment that they find peace in prayer. Finally I believe that at some future date the church in its wisdom will realize the unnecessary hurt that is being experienced by many who cannot in conscience continue to live a lie.[2]

The common sense of our culture is deeply hostile to traditional belief. To have the question of integrity put so articulately by the common man may not be entirely typical, and it may be less acutely felt by younger generations. Yet as I watch children grow up in today's world, what I see is joyful acceptance of religious stories and ideas in the infant schools, and progressive rejection in the junior schools, precisely because most religious teaching comes in the same category as Santa Claus. It is essential that the church on the ground takes critical questioning and investigation more seriously, that ordinands and preachers do not sit lightly to their training in academic theology, imagining that it is irrelevant. The church is in danger of becoming a sect of the credulous, simply because we do not value the proper childish activities of investigating what most interests us with boldness and enthusiasm.

Of course, there is a risk involved. Critical theology has undoubtedly got a bad press in the churches because so often it seems to undermine faith. Rock-climbers speak of hanging on to a cliff with their eyebrows when they find themselves in tight situations – and to some people it seems as if theologians have lost contact with the rock and are dangerously suspended over an abyss of uncertainty, clinging on to the unprovable with no more than their fingernails. Yet retreat is no solution. The only way is to press on. You are OK as long as the rock is the cliff-face, and not loose chippings or extraneous growth which is inherently unstable. In the end a secure stance will be discovered. Then you can make your belay and bring up others behind with safety. It is no good retreating from the challenge, running away from the questions, abusing those who are doing the weeding and cleaning up the climb. It is essential to take the expedition seriously enough to engage with the fundamental problems which it faces. It is no good pretending that the issues are not fundamental and serious. In today's world, they are. It is those who appeal to 'simple faith' who are living in an ivory tower, not those who risk a bad press by asking questions.

The church needs critical theology, and if it comes to that, critical theology needs the church. The breakdown in understanding is not one-sided – breakdowns in communication never are. It is not only the retreat from study in the churches that is deplorable; academic theology itself has been distorted, and is often misrepresented by its exponents. Scholarship has come to mean in many quarters a comprehensive knowledge of bibliographical material, acquaintance with the mass of books and articles published in modern times by lecturers looking for promotion. Academic achievement has come to be equated with the production of 'original' work, so that the budding researcher chases after new fashions, and second-rate articles arguing confidently for novel positions pour out from the presses. Too often teaching has become a judicious survey of recent work, as though the latest idea must be the most authoritative. It is hardly surprising that students get the impression that academic study is remote and irrelevant, a province to be left to the specialist. More and more people are getting concerned about the dead-end into which the historico-critical method seems to have led, and in their desperation abandon conventional approaches, preaching structuralism or some other ideology as the solution to the impasse; but too often that just creates another area of abstruse specialism. Once, scholarship meant soaking oneself in original texts, reflecting on their meaning and not rushing to conclusions, sitting humbly before the given. Once, originality meant the discovery and publication of new documents, or the pioneering work of their interpretation. Once, theology was a profound wrestling with the tradition by study of its great exponents. Academic theology, and perhaps biblical study in particular, needs to rediscover its own soul. The proliferation of groups dedicated to a corporate act of study and reflection, a revival of serious interest in learning the original languages in which the great treasures of the tradition have been written, a real engagement with the material and a communication of the excitement of such an endeavour – all this could do much to restore a proper sense of proportion in academic theology, and if it led to fewer abstruse articles being written and read, it might be no bad thing.

The chief thing is to make an acquaintance with an author, to wrestle with him and find out what he has to tell, or to teach, and when you have done with him, pass on to another and enrich yourself at his expense, but he will be none the poorer for all the wealth you may extract from his repository.[3]

Alfred Williams, the writer of those words, was a poet and a self-taught scholar who worked at Swindon Railway Works. He learned Greek by chalking it on the back of his steam hammer or the toes of his working-boots. He recited Homer and Horace as he tramped around the Wiltshire countryside. He had left school at eleven to become an odd-job boy on a farm, but by the end of his life he had mastered not only the Greek and Latin classics, but Sanskrit as well. For he was a seeker after the truths of the spirit and would leave no stone unturned. That is the kind of consuming passion for study which we need to rediscover.

Fruitful study depends upon people seeing the need and desiring to pursue it beyond anything else. Those who seek it are often people like Alfred Williams – over-stretched adults in evening classes or disadvantaged black church leaders – people who find it hard to make time or muster energy to pursue their interest. Yet those who have the opportunity to learn such things as Greek and Hebrew – students and especially ordinands – often dismiss these studies as irrelevant in the modern world. For a long time I have wanted to issue copies of an essay by Simone Weil to all half-hearted students. It is entitled 'Reflections on the Right Use of School Studies with a View to the Love of God'.[4] Here are some seminal sentences:

> The key to a Christian conception of studies is the realization that prayer consists of attention. It is the orientation of all the attention of which the soul is capable towards God. The quality of the attention counts for much in the quality of the prayer. Warmth of heart cannot make up for it . . .

Although people seem to be unaware of it today, the development of the faculty of attention forms the real object and almost the sole interest of studies. Most school studies have an intrinsic interest as well, but such an interest is secondary. All tasks which really call upon the power of attention are interesting for the same reason and to an almost equal degree . . .

If we have no aptitude or natural taste for geometry, this does not mean that our faculty of attention will not be developed by wrestling with a problem or studying a theorem. On the contrary, it is almost an advantage . . . Students must therefore work without any wish to gain good marks, to pass examinations, to win school successes; without reference to their natural abilities and tastes; applying themselves equally to all their tasks, with the idea that each one will help to form in them the habit of that attention which is the substance of prayer. When we set out to do a piece of work, it is necessary to wish to do it correctly, because such a wish is indispensable if there is to be true effort. Underlying this immediate objective, however, our deep purpose should aim solely at increasing the power of attention with a view to prayer . . .

Not only does the love of God have attention for its substance; the love of our neighbour, which we know to be the same love, is made of this same substance. Those who are unhappy have no need for anything in this world but people capable of giving them their attention. The capacity to give one's attention to a sufferer is a very rare and difficult thing; it is almost a miracle; it *is* a miracle. Nearly all those who think they have this capacity do not possess it. Warmth of heart, impulsiveness, pity are not enough . . .

Only he who is capable of attention can do this.

So it comes about that, paradoxical as it may seem, a Latin prose or a geometry problem, even though they are done wrong, may be of great service one day, provided we devote the right kind of effort to them. Should the occasion arise, they can one day make us better able to give someone in affliction exactly the help required to save him, at the supreme moment of his need . . .

Academic work is one of those fields which contain a pearl so precious that it is worth while to sell all one's possessions, keeping nothing for ourselves, in order to be able to acquire it.

These words were written by one deeply involved in the struggles of workers in the France of the 1930s; one who died in exile in England during the war, partly as a result of refusing to live a life more comfortable than that experienced by those in Occupied France. Academic study at its best is not retreating to an ivory tower, but learning to submit oneself to discipline, to the objectivity of a text, to the reality of other people's thoughts, to high standards of honesty and attention to detail, to a special kind of humility, to an ability to listen across the centuries and across cultural divergences for the accents of truth mediated through a diversity of forms.

Academic theology at its best is concerned with the central questions, not the proliferation of marginal theories. And the central questions are the fundamental questions about the faith which arise from the conditions of people's lives as they are lived – the commonsense questions about the reality and nature of

God, the problem of suffering, the meaning of prayer, the interpretation of scripture, the nature of religious language, the
purpose of worship, the relationship between the world inside
the church and the world outside in which people actually pass
their lives. Maybe there is nothing startlingly new or original to
say in these areas, but there is always an important process of
assimilation, of making one's own the insights of the tradition.
We cannot afford to give in to the solemn visage of someone
reverently and gingerly handling a holy tradition which he dare
not disturb, nor to the complacent and solipsistic grin of someone delighting in his personal salvation – though both are of the
utmost importance to the wholeness of Christian faith. As children growing to maturity, we need to ask and to wrestle with the
fundamental questions about meaning and truth. We need to
appropriate the tradition by studying it critically and yet with
respect.

If you have never met Anna, the six-year-old friend of Fynn,
you have missed a remarkable spiritual experience. The joy of
Anna is her awareness that all things issue from the mind of
Mister God; there is a wholeness in her response to life which is
simple and yet profound. Anna is the ideal child, and yet she is
vibrant with real life. Fynn describes her coming to meet him on
his way home from work.

Sometimes she would, without any words, just touch my hand
in greeting; sometimes the last few steps transformed her, she
let everything go with one gigantic explosion, and flung herself at me. So many times she would stop just in front of me
and hold out her closed hands. I learned rapidly what to expect on these occasions. It meant that she had found something that had moved her. We would stop and inspect
whatever the day's find was – perhaps a beetle, a caterpillar,
or a stone. We would look silently, heads bowed over today's
treasure. Her eyes were large deep pools of questions. How?
Why? What? I'd meet her gaze and nod my head; this was
enough, she'd nod in reply.

The first time this happened, my heart seemed to come off

its hook. I struggled to hold on. I wanted to put my arms round her to comfort her. Happily I managed to do the right thing . . . Unhappiness is to be comforted, and so perhaps too is fear, but these particular moments with Anna were moments of pure and undiluted wonder . . . I could not comfort her, I would not have dared to trespass. All that I could do was to see as she saw, to be moved as she was moved. That kind of suffering you must bear alone . . .

. . . then she launched forth.

'Mister God made everything, didn't he?'

There was no point in saying that I didn't really know. I said, 'Yes' . . .

She nodded her agreement. 'Does Mister God love us truly?'

'Sure thing', I said. 'Mister God loves everything.'

'Oh', she said. 'Well then, why does he let things get hurt and dead?' Her voice sounded as if she felt she had betrayed a sacred trust, but the question had been thought and it had to be spoken.

'I don't know', I replied. 'There's a great many things about Mister God that we don't know about.'

'Well then,' she continued, 'if we don't know a great many things about Mister God, how do we know he loves us?' . . .

She was silent for a little while. Later I thought that at this moment she was taking her last look at babyhood. Then she went on:

'Fynn, Mister God doesn't love us.' She hesitated. 'He doesn't really, you know, only people can love . . . I love you Fynn, and you love me, don't you?'

I tightened my arm about her.

'You love me because you are people. I love Mister God truly, but he don't love me.'

It sounded to me like a death-knell. 'Damn and blast', I thought. 'Why does this have to happen to people? Now she's lost everything.' But I was wrong. She had got both feet planted firmly on the next stepping-stone.

'No,' she went on, 'no, he don't love me, not like you do, it's different, it's millions of times bigger.'[5]

To ask questions is ultimately to be enriched. 'Therefore let us leave the elementary doctrine of Christ and go on to maturity' (Heb. 6.1). 'Solid food is for the mature' (Heb. 5.14), and we shall enjoy it only if we struggle through the weaning process, leaving the old securities, becoming again as little children prepared to explore and test and investigate, tirelessly asking questions, yet trustful that out of the dying process will come resurrection. Genuine commitment to hard study and thinking is not simply a negative activity. It is an endeavour which is desperately important for healthy life in the church. Yes, there are risks. Nothing will look precisely the same again. A kind of death is involved. But the dividends can and should be incalculable. It is those who have more fear than faith who cannot trust that resurrection will be the outcome of the process.

2

The Outstretched Arms

Christ nailed up might be more than a symbol of all pain. He might in very truth contain all pain. And a man standing on a hilltop with his arms outstretched, a symbol of a symbol, he too might be a reservoir of all the pain that ever was.

John Steinbeck, *To a God Unknown*[1]

The Spirit said to Moses' heart that he should make a type of the cross, and of the one coming to suffer . . . So . . . standing high above them all, he stretched out his arms, and as he did so Israel was victorious. But then, whenever he let them drop, they were slain. To what purpose is this tale? That they might know that they cannot be saved unless they hope in him.

Epistle of Barnabas xii.2–3 (cf. Ex. 17.8–13)

Growing up in the Methodism of a generation ago, I could hardly fail to be confronted during my teens with the preaching of the cross and the appeal to accept Christ as my Lord and Saviour. I responded. Yet for all the emotion, and the great Wesley hymns, persistent questions soon supervened. What sense did it make to speak of Christ dying for our sins? How could it make any difference to me if someone else died in my place centuries ago? Is that really what scripture said and meant? Grappling with the doctrine of the atonement arose directly out of a common Christian experience.

Years later I discovered the hollowness of traditional answers

21

to the problem of evil. How could I go on believing in a good creator of the world when faced with a firstborn child who was severely handicapped? To explain suffering and evil away as necessary for moral progress and development was no longer possible: here was one incapable of moral and spiritual response. Grappling with the problem of evil arose out of experience of the tragic element apparently built into life.

At the heart of Christian faith is an absurdity that is highlighted by the child's question: 'What are colds for?'; or Anna's perplexity: 'Well then, why does he let things get hurt and dead?' The love of God does not seem to measure up to life's experiences; and why should his love require the cross? Questions are inevitable unless we are content with glib nonsense.

So how are we to understand the cross? The arms outstretched – are they a demonstration of justice done, victory won, and life begun? Or are they a symbol of pain, anguish, and sin? Or are they a gesture of welcoming love? How could they possibly be any of these things, anyway? The questioning must begin at the centre of it all.

Clearly there are all kinds of things involved in trying to discover an adequate answer. It is never worthwhile to try and think in a vacuum; so it would be useful to review the standard answers offered by the tradition. After all, great Christian thinkers have wrestled with this one before we came on the scene. It would also be important to know what the Bible actually has to say on the matter, to consider how these statements are to be interpreted, how they are to be reinterpreted so as to make sense to us. This is where commitment to study comes in. We cannot face our questions by pure speculative thinking divorced from any consideration of those past contributions which have shaped the tradition as we have received it.

There have been a number of traditional ways of answering the question 'Why did Christ die?', of which two have become extremely important in the Western Christian tradition to which we belong. Both have their roots in the Middle Ages. The first is the theory of atonement that comes from one of the mediaeval archbishops of Canterbury, Anselm, who lived from about 1033 to 1109. His relations with the crown were stormy and uncomfortable, and as an uncompromising defender of the independence and authority of the church, he found himself in exile on several occasions. During one of these exiles he wrote a work of lasting influence and importance called *Cur Deus Homo?*: Why did God become man?

Many accounts of what Anselm wrote are to be found in standard textbooks, but there really is no substitute for going back to the text and reading it for oneself. That is what proper study involves. What follows – brief as it is – arises from my own excursion, and I certainly received a very different impression of the so-called Anselmian theory by taking the trouble to examine Anselm's own argument. It is an impressive argument, with a certain brilliant quality which arises from its cool logical progression from assumption to conclusion. Surprisingly, it is not in any way based on appeal to scripture. It was quite deliberately and self-consciously a rational and philosophical answer to the question why God became flesh, centring on the concept of justice.

The fundamental presupposition of Anselms' argument is that justice requires that sin be punished. Before God could forgive, the demands of justice had to be met; justice had to be satisfied. Thus the thesis of *Cur Deus Homo?* I.19 is: that man cannot be saved without satisfaction for sin. What distinguishes men from angels is the fact of sin, and unless sin is dealt with, man cannot be restored and made equal with the angels. What is meant by *satisfactio*? It means payment of the debt owed to God's justice. God cannot dismiss sin unpunished.

But at this point Anselm's second character in the dialogue intervenes: how then can we pray 'Forgive us our trespasses'? The answer, that that is precisely why Christ died, leads into the next thesis (I.20): that the satisfaction ought to be proportionate to the measure of sin, and man cannot make it for himself. Penance, abstinence, toils of the body, mercy and obedience – all these do nothing to make up for human sin because all this you ought to do anyway. Man cannot pay what he owes. The debt is so great that only God himself could pay it. So the incarnation

[margin note: man & angels]

[bottom margin note: God paid our debt!]

23

becomes a logical necessity for the resolution of man's problem, and the second book expounds this. God alone could pay the debt, since it was too great for man; man alone could pay the debt since he owed it: so only the God-Man could make the necessary satisfaction (II.6). Thus Christ had to be both God and Man, and his death (II.14) compensates for the sins of all men. He paid what was owed; he suffered the punishment due; he satisfied the abstract principle of justice and thus God was able to forgive sinful men. ~itself~

Jesus

Anselm's theory entered the Western heritage and sank deep into the Christian mind. Bunyan's *Pilgrim's Progress* bears witness to its penetration: take for example Christian's dialogue with Hope.

As I was looking for nothing but Hell and the everlasting damnation of my soul, suddenly, as I thought, I saw the Lord Jesus look down from heaven upon me and saying, *Believe in the Lord Jesus Christ, and thou shalt be saved.*

But I replyed, Lord, I am a great, a very great sinner; and he answered, *My grace is sufficient for thee* . . . Then the water stood in mine eyes, and I asked further, But Lord, may such a great sinner as I am, be indeed accepted of thee and be saved by thee? And I heard him say, *And him that cometh to me, I will in no wise cast out.* Then I said, But how, Lord, must I consider of thee in my coming to thee . . .

Then he said, *Christ Jesus came into the world to save sinners. He is the end of the Law for righteousness to everyone that believes. He died for our sins, and rose again for our justification : He loved us and washed us from our sins in his own blood : He is Mediator* between God and us. *He ever liveth to make intercession for us.* From all which I gathered, that I must look for righteousness in his person, and for satisfaction for my sins by his blood; that what he did in obedience to his Fathers Law, and in submitting to the penalty thereof was not for himself, but for him that will accept it for his salvation and be thankful. And now was my heart full of joy, mine eyes full of tears, and mine affections running over with love, to the Name, People and Ways of Jesus Christ.

Christian This was a revelation of Christ to your soul indeed: But tell me particularly what effect this had upon your spirit.

Hope It made me see that all the world, notwithstanding all the righteousness thereof, is in a state of condemnation. It made me see that God the Father, though he be just, can justly justify the coming sinner . . .

. . . had I now a thousand gallons of blood in my body, I could spill it all for the sake of the Lord Jesus.[2]

The theory penetrated deeply, and with varying degrees of sophistication, this understanding of atonement has remained that of conservative churchmen both catholic and evangelical. It has come to be known as the 'penal substitution' theory, though this description represents a slight shift in emphasis from that of Anselm himself; it implies that Christ bore our *punishment* rather than paying the debt due to God's honour – thus transferring the image from civil to criminal law. However, it is in this form that the theory has had its profound effect on popular Christianity, as well as on the exegesis of scripture. One only has to think of some popular hymns to discern its impact:

> There was no other good enough
>   To pay the price of sin;
> He only could unlock the gate
>   Of heaven and let us in.
>
> He dies to atone
>   For sins not his own;
> Your debt he has paid,
>   and your work he has done.

By the association of the biblical language of ransom and sacrifice with this 'penal' theory, a whole wealth of material has been pressed into its service:

O perfect redemption, the purchase of blood!
To every believer the promise of God,
The vilest offender who truly believes,
That moment from Jesus a pardon receives.

In fact, in its popular form, the theory has had powerful psychological and evangelical force because one who responds to it feels that something objective has been done to resolve the guilty situation in which he finds himself: Christ was punished in his stead to satisfy the demands of divine justice.

The fact that Anselm did justice to the psychological situation is the main reason why his doctrine was the most effective one, at least in Western Christianity ... For the believing Christian, this means that his consciousness of guilt is affirmed in its unconditional character. At the same time he feels the inescapability of that punishment which is nevertheless taken over by the infinite depth and value of the suffering of Christ. Whenever he prays that God may forgive his sins because of the innocent suffering and death of the Christ, he accepts both the demand that he himself suffer infinite punishment and the message that he is released from guilt and punishment by the substitutional suffering of the Christ. This point gave the Anselmian doctrine its strong psychological effect, and kept it alive in spite of its dated legalistic terminology and its quantitative measuring of sin and punishment. The discovery of an often deeply hidden guilt feeling has given us a new key for an explanation of the tremendous effect of the Anselmian theory on personal piety, hymns, liturgies, and much of Christian teaching and preaching. A system of symbols which gives the individual courage to accept himself in spite of his awareness that he is unacceptable has every chance to be accepted itself.[3]

At the level of feeling, I confess to being deeply sympathetic to this: the joy and freedom of realizing that responsibility for one's actions has been lifted, that guilt at failure to live up to the demands and ideals of the gospel is resolved, amazement at the gift of grace – that is part of my own evangelical experience.

26

Furthermore, this theory is deeply consonant with one of the profoundest insights of Christian theology, namely the doctrine of sin. The essential pride and self-sufficiency of humanity which challenges and denies God, boasts of its own achievements, refuses to submit, is recognized as a most serious issue, indeed the issue which most fundamentally affects the individual and the entire human race. That God cannot overlook or shrug off the state of mankind must be true; love, true love, is not sentimental and soppy, but demanding as well as accepting.

Our first theory of atonement, then, is an impressive one; arms outstretched in supplication to God, bearing the penalty for the sin of all. The cross is central and abidingly relevant because there a transaction was carried out which once and for all puts every person in a different position in relation to God, provided there has been a response in faith. It works at the popular level; it is capable of reasoned exposition. To question it is to tread on very sensitive territory, because it lies at the very heart of the faith of a great many people. Yet surely we cannot avoid asking questions about it. Does it not actually raise more difficulties than it solves?

The theory has a moral and legal basis. So you would expect it to be morally and legally satisfactory. But is it? Surely the substitution of an innocent victim for the guilty party does absolutely nothing to satisfy the claims of justice, at least, not as we usually understand it. Why should a criminal get off scot free while someone else pays the penalty? It will not do. Indeed, it is a gross travesty of justice against which we would all protest in any other context. How, then, can the theory work? Of course it is inspiring to reflect, 'Greater love has no man than this, that a man lay down his life for his friends.' It is appropriate to reflect on this in the context of war and self-sacrifice for others. But it will not do in a legal context.

Then there are theological problems raised by it. Is it not true that a concept of abstract justice actually determines the whole operation? And I mean *determines*. God has lost his freedom and sovereignty; he is bound by a principle. Why could he not just

27

choose to be merciful? After all, even earthly kings can do that. Why is he not free to do whatever he wills? The concept of God implied here is not consistent with the God of grace preached in the Evangelical Revival, nor with the God of sovereign freedom appealed to by Paul in Romans 9–11. So the theory is not consonant with other emphases in Christian theology; and there is an inherent contradiction, if not in Anselm's own presentation, at least in the way in which his argument has been utilized in other contexts.

Nor do the difficulties end there. Even though Anselm himself would deny this charge, this theory damages the unity of God and endangers trinitarian theology; for it implicitly sets the Father and the Son against each other. The Father tends to be characterized as just and wrathful, and the Son tends to be characterized as merciful and loving, voluntarily bearing in our stead the punishment inflicted by the Father. Such a doctrine cannot be defended. It is entirely out of tune with the consistent message of the New Testament: there we find Christ acting on God's behalf at every point, and salvation comes to mankind through God's initiative. God is the one who saves, Christ acts as Judge of the world. How then can it be maintained that forgiveness was made possible by the fact that the Son satisfied the Father's justice or appeased the Father's wrath?

Which leads us to the next difficulty. Defenders of this theory always appeal to scripture – indeed, they claim that scripture is its very basis. Yet study of Anselm's own work has highlighted its non-scriptural character. As far as Anselm is concerned, it is explicitly an argument based on *reason*: as far as modern commentators are concerned, it is a culturally determined argument deriving from the assumptions of the feudal society of mediaeval Europe in which Anselm lived and worked. As F. R. Barry put it, 'He thinks in terms of the reparation due for the slighted honour of man's supreme overlord – a due far greater than sinful man can pay.'[4] The then current understanding of penance as a way of making up for sin, and the then common practice of offering masses as sacrifices for sin, no doubt reinforced these presuppositions. In any case, whatever the reasons for it, *this theory was not in origin scriptural.* Subsequently scripture texts have been interpreted in the light of this theory, and the theory itself has become identified with the position of conservative evangelicals, for whom scripture is theoretically the only basis of doctrine. An impressive case for the scriptural basis of the theory is made by Leon Morris in *The Apostolic Preaching of the Cross*.[5] But in the light of what has been said earlier, can we avoid asking whether this theory really allows its exponents to appreciate what scripture is about? Does it not impose a foreign straight-jacket on its interpretation?

So why did Christ die? The first answer rooted in Western Christian tradition has strengths and weaknesses; what about the second? The second answer derives from a near contemporary of Anselm, named Abelard (1079–1142). Abelard is probably best known these days for his scandalous but beautiful love affair with Héloise, especially as popularized by Helen Waddell. In his own day he was a controversial figure quite apart from that; his brilliant and independent mind led him into one controversy after another. His students were wildly enthusiastic, but his colleagues did not appreciate his refutations of their carefully constructed positions. During a stormy life, he found himself condemned as a heretic and hounded from his monastery; yet he had enormous influence through his writings. At the time his philosophical position and his dialectical methods appeared most important: centuries later, it is his view of atonement which has kept his name alive in theological circles. Abelard's views have been espoused with enthusiasm by liberal Protestants of the nineteenth and twentieth centuries, largely because of dissatisfaction with the moral and theological implications of the Anselmian theory. Thus, for several generations, church life and theology have been affected by the existence of two traditions at loggerheads, producing different exegeses of scripture.

Abelard's view of atonement is relatively simple. The cross was a demonstration of God's love and grace; this demonstration calls forth our repentance so that we can be forgiven and return to obedience to God's will. As he puts it in his *Commentary on Romans*:

29

Each is also made more just, that is more loving of God, after the passion of Christ than before, because a benefit bestowed kindles more love than a benefit hoped for. So our redemption is that supreme love produced in us by the passion of Christ, which not only frees us from slavery to sin, but acquires for us the true liberty of sons of God; so that for love of him rather than from fear, we fulfil all things – love of him who has done us such a great favour that a greater cannot be found, he himself asserts: 'Greater love has no man than this that he lay down his life for his friends.'[6]

In the preceding section, Abelard offers criticisms of other ways of understanding the atonement. He refuses to accept that Christ was offered to the devil as a ransom-price, as indeed had Anselm; but he does not like the idea that he is offered to God either:

> To whom then does it not seem cruel and wicked that one requires the blood of an innocent victim and a ransom-price, or that in some other way the death of an innocent placates one? Yet God has accepted the death of his Son so as to be reconciled by it to the whole world . . . To us it seems that we are justified nonetheless in the blood of Christ and reconciled to God in this: that by this extraordinary grace exhibited to us, in that his Son assumed our nature and by teaching us by word and example persevered unto death, he draws us closer to himself through love; so that fired by so great a benefit of divine grace, there is nothing your love for him would dread facing . . .
> I think therefore that the purpose and cause of the incarnation was that he might illuminate the world with the light of his wisdom, and kindle it to love of himself.[7]

Repentance is produced by contemplation of the cross; love is generated in us in response to God's demonstration of love on the cross.

Now this, too, is a powerful view of the effect of the cross. It worked for Abelard himself, as is evidenced by one of his letters to Héloise. The letter was written when both were well-established in religious communities. Their secret marriage had been destroyed years before by the thugs employed to castrate Abelard; at his command, Héloise had entered the convent of which she was now prioress. After years without contact, she suddenly came across a copy of Abelard's account of his ongoing struggles, and wrote a desperate letter, revealing her continued love for Abelard and the impossibility, for her, of repenting of their love, its goodness and its joy. Abelard in the course of his reply writes:

Come too, my inseparable companion, and join me in thanksgiving, you who were made my partner both in guilt and in grace . . .

Are you not moved to tears or remorse by the only-begotten Son of God who, for you and for all mankind, in his innocence was seized by the hands of impious men, dragged along and scourged, blindfolded, mocked at, buffeted, spat upon, crowned with thorns, finally hanged between thieves on the cross, at the time so shameful a gibbet, to die a horrible and accursed form of death? Think of him always, sister, as your true spouse of all the Church . . . Look at him going to be crucified for your sake, carrying his own cross . . . Have compassion on him who suffered willingly for your redemption, and look with remorse on him who was crucified for you . . . He bought and redeemed you with his own blood. See what right he has over you, and know how precious you are . . . What has he seen in you, I ask you, when he lacks nothing, to make him seek even the agonies of a fearful and inglorious death in order to purchase you? . . . He is the true friend who said when he was about to die for you: 'There is no greater love than this, that a man should lay down his life for his friends.' It was he who truly loved you, not I. My love, which brought us both to sin, should be called lust, not love . . . You say I suffered for you, and perhaps that is true, but it was really *through* you, and even this unwillingly; not for love of you but under compulsion, and to bring you not salvation but

sorrow. But he suffered truly for your salvation, on your behalf, of his own free will, and by his suffering he cures all
sickness and removes all suffering. To him, I beseech you, not
to me, should be directed all your devotion, all your compassion, all your remorse. Weep for the injustice of the great
cruelty inflicted on him, not for the just and righteous payment
demanded of me.[8]

Abelard's understanding of the cross is more powerful than it
is sometimes given credit for. Love poured out in death does
have a compelling effect. The price of love was high. This again
has an impact which can be clearly seen by looking at the hymns
that are deeply engrained in our tradition:

> See from his head, his hands, his feet,
> Sorrow and love flow mingled down:
> Did e'er such love and sorrow meet,
> Or thorns compose so rich a crown.

> My song is love unknown,
> My Saviour's love to me;
> Love to the loveless shown,
> That they might lovely be.
>   O who am I
>   That for my sake
>   My Lord should take
>   Frail flesh and die?

Another powerful understanding of the cross, then – arms
stretched out to demonstrate the breadth and depth of God's
love for each and everyone of us. For many that is sufficient
explanation. But is it adequate?

The most common criticism of this view is that it is purely
'subjective'. All it effects is man's *response* to God's act of love.
The cross, seen in these terms, did not make any objective difference to the situation. For this reason many regard it as totally
inadequate as a theory because it reduces the cruciality of the
cross. Actually, that may be no bad thing! After all, what about
the people who lived *before* the event? And how could the

forgiveness proclaimed by Jesus during his life be dependent on his future sacrifice? Overemphasis on the cruciality of the cross raises all kinds of difficulties. Yet there is something in the objection nevertheless: if the cross did not actually effect something new, if it made no *real* difference, if it did not establish a different relationship between God and man, why was it necessary? Does not forgiveness become cheap grace? Is there not a danger of sentimentality? Maybe it is true that

> this love awakens in man the answering love which is certain that, in God, love, not wrath, is the last word. But this is not sufficient to take away the anxiety about guilt and the feeling of having to undergo punishment. The violated justice cannot be re-established by the message of the divine love alone . . . In so far as the predominantly subjective description of the process of atonement misses this point, it could not be accepted as adequate by Christian theology.[9]

The resolution of guilt needs more than a loving demonstration that the hurt does not matter. For 'justice is the structural form of love without which it would be sheer sentimentality'. Respect is lost on both sides if offences are shrugged off.

And there is another problem: this kind of view drastically oversimplifies the very complex statements made about the meaning of the cross in the New Testament. The language of sacrifice and ransom, justification and redemption, is taken in a very much weakened sense, or nowadays dismissed as culturally relative and no longer applicable. So once again, the relationship between a theory and its scriptural roots is problematic.

Why did Christ die? So far we have observed two traditional answers, often co-existing in the life of the churches, but in theory and in argument deeply opposed to one another, particularly since the work of liberal Protestants, culminating in the Bampton lectures of Hastings Rashdall, pressed the objections to the Anselmian theory and took up Abelard instead. On the conservative side, reasoned attempts had already been made to defend the 'penal substitution' theory, notably by R. W. Dale and J. Denney. In fact, from the 1870s to the 1930s the doctrine of atonement was at the centre of theological interest; its history was written and re-written in defence of one view or the other.[10] So positions on atonement became polarized by their association with the wider liberal-conservative struggle, and debate over the proper interpretation of key texts of scripture tended to proceed along party lines. This has to some extent remained the case. Yet both positions are problematic; for, as we have seen, both give rise to serious questions if one really examines them and thinks them through. Can anything be done to resolve the difficulties, lessen the polarization, find an alternative, or discover deeper insight?

Well, an alternative has been proposed, and it evoked a very considerable response for a period. Just before the last war, a Swedish scholar, Gustaf Aulen, pointed out that neither of the two theories we have examined so far really goes back to the early church at all.[11] The fundamental view that we find in the early church, and indeed in Luther, is of a quite different kind. Aulen called it the 'classic theory', thus claiming for it what he saw as its proper status as the perennial and central view never entirely submerged in the history of the church. That he was right in his judgment is surely confirmed by the fact that both Anselm and Abelard found it necessary to dismiss this view before proceeding further with the discussion.

What Aulen observed was that the very varied and diverse language of the Fathers of the church resolves itself into a single basic perception: a cosmic battle between good and evil, God and Satan, in which the cross was the decisive moment of victory. Christians were seen as still engaged in the struggle, now reduced to something more like a mopping-up operation. Salvation, for the Fathers, was liberation from a world possessed by demons, the destruction of sorcery and magic, ignorance and superstition, the conquest of sin and death, the end of mental and physical corruption. This was achieved by rescuing man from the clutches of the devil, a rescue effected by the cross. The blood of Christ was paid as a ransom to the devil to free mankind from enslavement to him. Some of the Fathers even suggested that God deliberately tricked the devil, just like a fisherman put-

34

ting tempting bait on the end of a fishing-line. (After all, Christ said, 'I am a worm and no man', at least if you presuppose, as the Fathers did on the basis of Mark 15.34, that all the words of Ps. 22 belong to Christ.) Thus, the devil was tempted to swallow up the human Jesus in death, but then discovered that he could not stomach this morsel because Christ was sinless. So Christ arose and the devil was foiled. A slightly less crude explanation of the payment made to the devil was based on the idea that man had sold himself to the devil by his sin, and therefore the devil had rights over man. Now you may find such pictures amusing, but you are likely to reject them as so primitive and crude as to be utterly unacceptable, no matter how distinguished their ancestry. Quite clearly the whole notion belongs to an old mythological story of conflict between God and the powers of evil, and there are not many who are likely to find it attractive or intellectually acceptable these days. If we take God's primacy and uniqueness seriously, it will not do to suggest that there is a powerful demonic being alongside God capable of foiling his purposes, quite apart from the fact that the devil and all his angels have for the most part (though not entirely) been 'de-mythologized' within the churches of the modern Western world. So you may be wondering how Aulen's 'classic theory' won any kind of hearing in the twentieth century. Why drag up something that even mediaevals like Anselm and Abelard had dismissed on rational and theological grounds?

The answer lies in the context, the situation within which Aulen's book appeared. Liberalism was given a nasty shock by the events of the 1930s and 1940s. In the second half of the twentieth century, people are far more aware of the problem that evil is deeply resistant to human efforts to root it out – moral progress has not in fact gone in step with material and scientific progress. We are trapped in what has been called the 'total nexus of evil' in the world – the political, social and economic forces that bind us, our own heredity and environment, our own unconscious drives and the 'system'. Violence and injustice are institutionalized. Individuals get caught up in social and economic conflicts; almost unawares, they are sucked into mass movements which effect destruction and spread hate. We are responsible and yet not responsible. We fashion the structures of society and yet are enslaved by them. There is a kind of demonic power evident in society and in history – indeed within ourselves, even if we would not naturally think of it as a personal devil. So Aulen stimulated several profound attempts to rediscover and re-present in acceptable modern terms the notion that the cross was God's final victory over the power of evil in the world. The extent of Aulen's influence is apparent to anyone who looks at H. A. Hodges, *The Pattern of Atonement* or *Death and Life Have Contended*, or the work of F. R. Barry on *The Atonement*. The theory is also sensitively interpreted, along with many other approaches, in F. W. Dillistone's major study, *The Christian Understanding of Atonement*. Besides, the extent to which this kind of dualist thinking affects the New Testament itself is now commonplace: a notable study is R. Leivestad, *Christ the Conqueror*.[12]

Certainly the impact of this kind of thinking in the early church is undeniable. Not everyone dwelt on the cruder, mythological aspects: Athanasius, for example, was capable of producing a highly sophisticated account of atonement in terms of victory with hardly a mention of the devil: I refer to the *De Incarnatione*, another classic work of Christian theology which repays careful study. (See also my *Sacrifice and the Death of Christ*, ch. 5.)[13] What the early Fathers of the church were deeply aware of was the fact that man's problem is not just sin – it is not just a moral problem, as the Western approaches to atonement tend to assume. There is something in the present constitution of creation as a whole which is corrupt. Sin is one symptom of a deeper problem – the problem of ignorance, weakness and sheer powerlessness, the problem of perversity, the problem of sickness, decay and death – the profound resistance of man and his environment to full and enduring life and peace. The prevailing response to all this in the ancient world was a search for power to overcome corruption and mortality – some found it in magic, some in philosophy. Others found it in the Christian gospel, the good news of victory over sin, death and the devil. Ideas about salvation and atonement were inseparable from the total problem of evil – indeed the gospel was the 'solution' to the problem of evil, if not in theory, at least in practice. The cross was a symbol of triumph – arms outstretched to ensure that the battle went God's way, a banner under which the church continued the fight against all forms of evil – idolatry, heresy, sorcery, sin, and above all death. Look up Exodus 17.8–13; then turn to the head of this chapter, and remembering the context just sketched, reflect on the quotation from the *Epistle of Barnabas*. Imagine the impact of this story of Moses, interpreted as a type, a prophetic symbol, of Christ on the cross. The martyr and the monk forsook all to engage in the battle on the side of Christ, trusting that effective victory was already won by the triumph of Christ on the cross. Nor has this response to the cross entirely died. Think of the hymn:

> Lift high the cross, the love of Christ proclaim
> Till all the world adore his sacred name.
>
> Come brethren, follow where our Captain trod,
> Our King victorious, Christ the Son of God:
>
> Led on their way by this triumphant sign,
> The hosts of God in conquering ranks combine:
>
> Each new-born soldier of the Crucified
> Bears on his brow the seal of him who died:
>
> O Lord, once lifted on the glorious Tree,
> As thou hast promised, draw men unto thee.

This relatively modern hymn picks up the images of the early church; the new-born soldier was the convert newly-baptized, and the seal on his brow he received in baptism. Thus he joined God's army and donned his armour to follow Christ's standard into battle.

This understanding of the cross has not been confined to the early church and its imitators; indeed, Aulen's study gave particular attention to Luther. He claimed that really this sense of victory over sin and death was far more truly Luther's view than the 'penal substitution' tradition adopted by subsequent

37

Protestantism. It is interesting to see that this is born out by the
Luther hymns that have found a place in English tradition:

> A safe stronghold our God is still,
>   A trusty shield and weapon,
> He'll help us clear from all the ill
>   That hath us now o'ertaken.
>   The ancient prince of hell,
>   Hath risen with purpose fell;
>   Strong mail of craft and power
>   He weareth in this hour,
> On earth is not his fellow.
>
> With force of arms we nothing can,
>   Full soon were we down-ridden;
> But for us fights the proper Man
>   Whom God himself has bidden.
>   Ask ye: Who is this same?
>   Christ Jesus is his name,
>   The Lord Sabaoth's Son;
>   He and no other one
> Shall conquer in the battle.
>
> It was a strange and dreadful strife,
>   When Life and Death contended.
> The victory remained with Life,
>   The reign of death was ended:
>   Stript of power, no more he reigns;
> An empty form alone remains;
>   His sting is lost for ever.
>   Hallelujah.

Nor is it just Luther. This theme too has found a more widespread place in Christian tradition, particularly in popular
Easter hymns:

> Love's redeeming work is done,
> Fought the fight, the battle won;

38

The strife is o'er, the battle done;
Now is the Victor's triumph won;
The powers of death have done their worst
But Christ their legions hath dispersed.

His foes and ours were one,
Satan, the world and sin.
But he shall tread them down
And bring his kingdom in.

Given all this, has Aulen's initiative helped to resolve the impasse we noticed earlier? It certainly has drawn attention to an area of Christian thinking that found no place in the two theories that had become traditional. It has broadened the scope of the discussion, showing that atonement is not just to do with sin, but with the whole complex of evil in the world. Yet profound weaknesses afflict this view too when it is turned into an overall theory. Long ago the idea that God deceived the devil, or that the devil had rights which God had to respect, came in for theological criticism. Both ideas are incompatible with a proper doctrine of God, since they imply that he is either immoral or not omnipotent. Indeed, the whole basis of this view of atonement rests on an unacceptable dualism. Is God really in long-term conflict with a comparable power working against his purposes? If so, he is not really God. Furthermore, we have already commented upon the fact that its fundamentally 'primitive' and 'mythological' character is not very attractive in the thought-world of today – we simply cannot take it seriously. But there is a more important objection: even if we 'de-mythologize' it, it is impossible to proclaim with any confidence that the cross of Christ has made the slightest difference to the situation. The world is *still* caught in the eternal struggle between good and evil. What use then asserting that in principle the victory was won on the cross? It does not appear to have been very effective.

So not one of these overall theories measures up to the kind of questions we feel constrained to ask if we are to get to the bottom of this central issue: why did Christ die, and what has it got to do with me? Each draws attention to some very important aspect

39

of the matter, but none does justice to the whole, none accounts
for the total impact that the cross has upon people, its constant
drawing power, its power as an evocative symbol, its ability to
make people sense here the solution to all that is wrong with the
world. Release from guilt through hearing the good news that
Jesus paid the penalty for us is a frequent and genuine Christian
experience; repentance before the revelation of God's love is a
quite genuine Christian response; the sense of hope and renewal
because God has overcome evil in oneself and in the world is
undeniably given to the Christian believer. Each theory gives
primacy to one of these responses; it does part of the job. It
cannot do justice to the whole.

Broaden the discussion to the impact of the cross outside the
church, in literature, in art, and the inadequacy of the theories is
even more apparent. At the head of this chapter, there is a striking sentence from a novel by John Steinbeck; his point about
the cross being a symbol of pain is graphically brought out in
another novel by a Jew, Chaim Potok, called *My name is Asher
Lev*. Remember, for the Jewish people the crucifix is the sign of
persecution, of death and suffering, the banner of the enemy: for
throughout Christian history, Christians have persecuted Jews.
In his story Potok tells of a Jewish boy with a gift for drawing
and painting; but he was born into a Hasidic community which,
in line with the Old Testament prohibition of images, could not
accept any kind of pictorial representation. The book is a story
of anguish, of deep conflict between him and his family, between
his family and the community in which he had to live. It ends
with him painting his mother on a crucifix, and as he does so he
says:

> For all the pain you suffered, my mama. For all the torment of
> your past and future years, my mama. For all the anguish this
> picture of pain will cause you. For the unspeakable mystery
> that brings good fathers and sons into the world and lets a
> mother watch them tear at each other's throats. For the
> Master of the Universe, whose suffering world I do not com-
> prehend. For dreams of horror, for nights of waiting, for

memories of death, for the love I have for you, for all things
I remember, and for all the things I should remember but
have forgotten, for all these I created this painting – an observ-
ant Jew working on a crucifix because there was no aesthetic
mould in his own religious tradition into which he could pour
a painting of ultimate anguish and torment.[14]

Now the theories hardly take any account of this aspect of the
cross – arms outstretched as a symbol of pain and suffering. Of
course, in Christian spirituality, the suffering of Christ has
always been a paradigm for Christian living and Christian suffering, quite apart from its atoning significance. All through Christian history, people have spoken of 'bearing their cross' and of
imitating the patience of Christ. The thought of Christ sharing
our agonies has been of enormous devotional power:

> O love divine, that stooped to share
>   Our sharpest pang, our bitterest tear.

> God is love: and he enfoldeth
>   All the world in one embrace;
> With unfailing grasp he holdeth
>   Every child of every race.
> And when human hearts are breaking
>   Under sorrow's iron rod,
> Then they find that self-same aching
>   Deep within the heart of God.

But in thinking theologically about atonement and its meaning, less than justice has been done to this in the past. I think
there are signs that Christian reflection on the atonement is turning more to this aspect of the cross, that there is more focus now
on pain and suffering as well as the problems of sin and evil.
This relates no doubt to the fact that modern theology has had
to face up to the fact that the problem of suffering and evil poses
the biggest question-mark against Christian claims about the
existence of a God of love who created this world. It is also one
of the fruits of Aulen's resuscitation of the 'classic theory'. But

perhaps more important, it has potential for deepening and widening the discussion, and doing more justice to the complexity of it all.

In the New Testament and in Christian tradition, there is a tremendous wealth of different responses to the cross, both at the thinking and the feeling level. All this is not reducible to any one single theory, or even some kind of combination of all of them. None of the traditional theories has proved satisfactory; none is adequate on its own. There is a very real sense in which a large notice has been put up against all the theories saying 'No through road'. If we are going to understand the meaning of the cross, then I suspect that we have to move outside the attempt to construct a theory. Perhaps if we probe a little further into the New Testament we may rediscover elements that have got obscured, forgotten or misinterpreted in the process of constructing theories. After all, we have suggested over and over again that adequate treatment of the complexity of scriptural ideas has been lacking in the theories we have explored.

So to scripture let us turn our attention.

3

The Woman in Travail

We know that the whole creation has been groaning in travail together until now; and not only the creation, but we ourselves, who have the first-fruits of the Spirit, groan inwardly as we wait for adoption as sons, the redemption of our bodies. For in this hope we were saved (Rom. 8.22-24a).

When we turn to scripture, the temptation is to begin by tackling the obvious controversial texts that have been slung back and forth in discussions of atonement. Does *hilastērion* in Romans 3.25 mean 'propitiation' or 'expiation'? What is the implication of the phrase 'the blood of Christ'? Does sacrificial language imply substitution? But let us resist that temptation for the moment. In the previous chapter it was suggested that one trouble with the theories is that they fasten on the texts which fit, and fail to do justice to the wider range of scriptural images and biblical understanding as a whole. If there is one thing that has emerged from our initial study, it is that the meaning of the cross must be related in some way not just to sin, but to all suffering, all pain, all disaster, all injustice, all decay and death – indeed to all that is wrong with the creation, human nature and human society as we know it. If atonement is to do with all that, *Paul* where better to start than with Paul's words in Romans 8 about the redemption of the whole creation which has been groaning in travail? *Romans*

Paul is clearly speaking of cosmic agony and the original Greek implies a particular image of agony which has a long history in the prophetic tradition: it is the pain of labour, the agony of a woman giving birth. As usual in biblical study, much can be learned by tracking down background material, and to explore the variations on this image is to observe an important dynamic in biblical thought. No student of the Bible can work without a concordance, the essential tool for identifying relevant passages; so using the concordance to start us off, let us examine those texts which speak of labour and childbirth.

Chronologically speaking, the first occurrence of the image is to be found in Hosea 13. In an oracle of judgment, God declares that Israel is to be destroyed. He has given Israel kings in anger, and taken them away in wrath – yet nothing succeeds in bringing the nation to repentance. So the record of Ephraim's sin is all tied up, and he is lost because he did not take the chance of birth into new hope:

> When the pangs of his birth came over his mother,
> He showed himself a senseless child;
> for at the proper time he could not present himself
> at the mouth of the womb (Hos. 13.13; NEB).

As it stands in its context, the verse is at first sight rather obscure; in my paraphrase of the context, links have been supplied to provide a sequence of thought, as also in the NEB's paraphrastic translation of the verse. Yet with that warning against over-confidence, we can surely deduce that failure to be born is an image of judgment. The image here focusses not primarily on the travailing mother, but on the unborn child who is not prepared to take advantage of the new life offered through repentance. This will prove to be an unusual use of the image, but a somewhat similar thought occurs on the lips of Hezekiah (II Kings 19.3/Isa. 37.3): 'This day is a day of distress, of rebuke, and of disgrace; children have come to the birth, and there is no strength to bring them forth.' Failure in the delivery of the child is a mark of judgment, the end of hope, as it is in Hosea's prophecy.

When we turn to Micah, the application of the image takes up the other side of the coin, so to speak. The stress is on the painful travail of the mother in labour. 'Writhe and groan, O daughter of Zion, like a woman in travail' (4.10). The image focusses on the agony of the condemned city. God is to give her up, for the time that a woman struggles in labour (5.3). This usage is the one which predominates. In the book of Isaiah, for example, it is associated with the Day of the Lord, the day of destruction: everyone is to be dismayed. Pangs and agony will seize them: they will be in anguish like a woman in labour (13.8). The difference is that here the image is in an oracle against Babylon, not Israel. This may be an important clue to its original use: in Ps. 48.6 the enemies of Israel are described as coming against Zion; but 'as soon as they saw it, they were astounded, they were in panic, they took flight; trembling took hold of them there, anguish as of a woman in travail.' In recent studies, important links have been traced between the psalms and the prophets; both seem to reflect traditional cultic forms.[1] Perhaps this image originated as a convention to be used in oracles against the nations and was then transposed by application to Israel's plight at the coming of judgment – after all, it is well established that Amos recast such oracles so as to turn them against Israel, and transformed hopeful expectations of the Day of the Lord into dire warnings of judgment. Perhaps a similar transformation has taken place in the particular case of this image.

It is in the book of Jeremiah that we find the image in most frequent use to refer to the pains brought on by the judgment of God:

> I heard a cry as of a woman in travail,
>   anguish as of one bringing forth her first child,
>   the cry of the daughter of Zion gasping for breath,
>   stretching out her hands,
>   'Woe is me! I am fainting before murderers' (4.31).

The enemy approaches from the north:

> We have heard the report of it,
>   our hands fall helpless;
> anguish has taken hold of us,
>   pain as of a woman in travail (6.24).

> Lift up your eyes and see
>   those who come from the north . . .
> Will not pangs take hold of you,
>   like those of a woman in travail (13.20–21).

> We have heard a cry of panic,
>   of terror and no peace.
> Ask now, and see,
>   can a man bear a child?
> Why then do I see every man
>   with his hands on his loins like a woman in labour?
> Why has every face turned pale? (30.5b–6).

In these passages, as in Micah's prophecy, Israel or Zion is like the woman in labour. But elsewhere, as in Isaiah, the image is used of other victims of God's judgment, perhaps confirming the suggestion that this was its original context:

> O inhabitants of Lebanon,
>   rested among the cedars,
> Now will you groan when pangs come upon you,
>   pain as of a woman in travail (22.23).

> Damascus has become feeble, she turned to flee,
>   and panic seized her;
> anguish and sorrows have taken hold of her,
>   as of a woman in travail (49.24).

> The king of Babylon heard the report of them,
>   and his hands fell helpless;
> anguish seized him,
>   pain as of a woman in travail (50.43).

So we have noticed two variations on the image: first, failure to deliver the child, or failure on the child's part to come to birth,

46

is seen as a mark of judgment and the end of hope for the future; secondly, the agonies of the condemned or the defeated, whether the experience of Israel's enemies or of Israel herself, is graphically depicted in terms of the pangs of a woman in labour. In one passage these two aspects of the image appear fused together:

> Like a woman with child,
>> who writhes and cries out in her pangs,
>> when she is near her time,
> So were we because of thee, O Lord;
>> we were with child, we writhed,
>> we have as it were brought forth wind (Isa. 26.17–18).

Here in the section known as the Isaiah apocalypse, the travail of God's people is depicted in terms of the woman in labour and judgment is associated with failure to produce a child. The dependence of this section on the book of Hosea has been recently argued,[2] and certainly Isaiah 24–27 appears to derive from post-exilic re-working of the prophetic tradition. So explicit fusing of the two variations may represent a late development. Be that as it may, clearly in the prophetic books the predominant thrust of the image, in whatever guise, is to highlight the pain, agony and hopelessness of those subject to destruction as a result of God's judgment.

However, that is not the only application. In Isaiah 21, the prophet himself appears to suffer anguish:

> Therefore my loins are filled with anguish;
>> pangs have seized me,
>> like the pangs of a woman in travail . . .
> My mind reels, horror has appalled me . . . (Isa. 21.3–4).

Why the prophet should feel such dismay, apparently at the fall of Babylon, is at first sight a puzzle, but it may simply be a way of expressing his terrified outcry in response to the awesome revelation received (cf. Hab. 3.16). In another surprising passage in Deutero–Isaiah, outcry in contrast to previous silence appears to be the principle thrust of the image. The context, it is thought,[3] is God's response through the prophet to the lament

47

of the community, its complaint that God is absent, silent, inactive, the kind of thing expressed in Isaiah 64.12. Here is the divine reply:

> The Lord goes forth like a mighty man . . .
> He cries out, he shouts aloud . . .
> For a long time I have held my peace,
> I have kept still and restrained myself;
> Now I will cry out like a woman in travail,
> I will gasp and pant . . .
> And I will lead the blind in a way that they know not,
>   in paths that they have not known I will guide them.
> I will turn the darkness before them into light,
>   the rough places into level ground.
> These are the things I will do, and I will not forsake them.
>
> (Isa. 42.14–16).

This use of the image stands out as unusual in two respects, first in that God is likened to the woman in travail, and secondly in that the cry is not the cry of pain and terror, but the gasping sound of labour and struggle. Although this is not explicitly stated, nor is there any indication that the prophet thought of God as travailing in the sense of suffering, the ensuing verses possibly imply that this labour of God's is a labour to bring forth a new people, restoration, new life, new hope. It is interesting that elsewhere the Hebrew verb for a woman giving birth, and travailing in the process, is used of God bearing Israel and giving birth to his own people (Deut. 32.18). Certainly here the image is used in a context of hope rather than judgment.

Nor is this the only time that the hope context is found. Jeremiah 31.8 is perhaps not all that significant: it was natural enough that those to be redeemed should include the blind, the lame, the pregnant woman and the woman in labour – presumably this list refers figuratively to Israel, so often depicted as being in such pitiful states. But potentially the image itself had 'hope' connotations, and these occasionally surfaced. In Micah 5.3, the fact that God is to give up Israel 'only so long as a woman is in labour' (NEB), implies that an end will come to the

pain. That the NEB is correct in adopting this sense is indicated
by the context: Micah 5.3b speaks of 'the rest of the brethren'
returning 'to the people of Israel'. It is in Trito–Isaiah, however,
that the image takes on a dramatically hopeful role:

> Jerusalem gives birth *before* being in labour
> She is delivered of a son *before* her pains come upon her
> (Isa. 66.7).

The passage is one of rejoicing because new life, new hope, new
birth is the emphasis rather than the preceding pain and agony
which is so prominent in most of the passages we have looked
at. Zion's success in giving birth, and doing so painlessly, is in
marked contrast to the passage in the Isaiah Apocalypse noted
earlier.

It is this dimension of *hope* which is strikingly taken up in
the New Testament. Its clearest expression is to be found in
John 16.21–22:

> When a woman is in travail she has sorrow, because her hour
> has come, but when she is delivered of the child, she no longer
> remembers the anguish, for joy that a child is born into the
> world. So you have sorrow now, but I will see you again and
> your hearts will rejoice, and no one will take your joy from
> you.

Here the image appears in the context of the Farewell Dis-
courses and is applied to the disciples' distress at parting with
Jesus; but reunion with him is a realistic hope, because the joy
of birth follows the pain of labour. One gets the impression that
this is in fact a sophisticated re-application of the statement
made in the key verse; for elsewhere the image appears in
apocalyptic contexts. Here the underlying pattern of ideas is
that a period of woes and tribulations, persecutions and wars, is
to be followed by the arrival of God's Kingdom or the Parousia
of the Lord Jesus – in other words, the sufferings of the present
time are the birth-pangs of a new age or a new creation. In Mark
13.8, the Greek word for 'labour-pains' is actually used: a list of
'Messianic woes' is called 'the beginning of the birth-pangs'

(Matt. 24.8). This is not always so explicitly drawn out, but look at I Thessalonians 5. The topic is the Day of the Lord:

> When the people say, 'There is peace and security', then sudden destruction will come upon them as travail comes upon a woman with child, and there will be no escape.

As in the prophets, the travail is here associated with the pain and anguish of judgment. But the passage as a whole points to the salvation to be expected because of our Lord Jesus Christ, who 'died for us so that whether we wake or sleep, we might live with him'. Look also at Revelation 12. The woman is in labour, crying out in anguish; but she gives birth to the Messiah who is caught up to God and to his throne. Whether any precise application of the image should be sought in this passage is a matter of considerable controversy: is it Mary? is it Jerusalem? who is it? Maybe precision of that sort is not intended – maybe the emphasis is upon the birth taking place, the fact of hope beyond the anguish, that judgment is not the end. There is a striking parallel in the Dead Sea Scrolls:

> I am in distress
> like a woman in travail with her firstborn,
> when her pangs come,
> and grievous pain on her birth-stool,
> causing torture in the crucible of the pregnant one;
> for sons have come to the waves of death,
> and she who conceived a man suffers in her pains;
> for in the waves of death she gives birth to a man-child;
> with pains of Sheol he bursts forth
> from the crucible of the pregnant one,
> a wonderful counsellor with his power.[4]

Note here the close association of the birth of new life and bursting from Sheol, which no doubt alludes to resurrection. As we shall note shortly, the two ideas are closely related in the New Testament.

So back to Romans 8.22: through prophecy and its reinterpretation in apocalyptic, the image of the woman in travail was associated with judgment, but potentially implied hope – the hope that out of the judgment, the afflictions, the dreadful events preceding the End, would be born a new creation, a new Messianic king, restoration and new life. From application to Israel and her chequered history, the image moves on to a cosmic stage. And here Paul thinks of God's dealings with the whole of creation in terms of this pattern: the whole creation groans and travails because it is under judgment, but the judgment itself is potentially a cause for hope – for the travail is the birth-pangs of a new age, a new people of God, a new creation.

> For I reckon that the sufferings of this present age are not worth considering compared with the glory about to be revealed to us. For the creation awaits with eager expectation the revelation of the sons of God (perhaps meaning their appearance through successful birth?). For the creation was subjected to vanity (decay, death, futility, hopelessness, failure), not willingly but through the one who did the subjecting and did it *in hope*, because even the creation itself will be rescued from slavery to decay into the glorious freedom of the children of God. For we know that all the creation is groaning and suffering labour-pains, right up to the present; and not only this, but we ourselves also who have the first-fruits of the Spirit, we too groan within ourselves expecting our adoption, the liberation of our bodies. For we were saved by hope (my translation).

This dimension of hope seems to me to be absolutely fundamental to the thinking of the New Testament writers. They were prepared to face suffering and persecution themselves because it was all part of the birth-pangs of the new age, the coming of the kingdom. Already in certain respects, they were experiencing an anticipation of this through the presence of the Spirit in their midst. They knew they were to be the community of saints who would survive the terrible woes, the awful pains of judgment which must come upon all creation. So they were saved in hope.

Now how does the death of Christ fit into this perspective? What meaning did it carry in the context of such expectations?

Well, it was a clear sign that the judgment had begun; the tribulations and woes, the sufferings and pains, were initiated by his submission to death. It was the beginning of the dreadful but final conflict with the powers of evil. So the Christian believer was living in a kind of tension between the present evil age and the world to come. The final judgment had begun, the kingdom was on the point of breaking in, and the resurrection of Christ was the first-fruits of the final resurrection. The suffering of Christ and the suffering that Christians were undergoing were the birth-pangs of a new age. Thus it was that the Christians could live in hope, and bear their suffering and their persecution with confidence. In Christ, God had begun to move with power. Christian faith was faith in one who had raised Christ from the dead, and therefore they could persevere with hope and confidence, joy and expectation.

So we can see now how fundamental to the hope of the early Christians was the whole death-resurrection drama. Interestingly enough, the development of the image we have explored is closely paralleled by the development of the resurrection-hope, and the two coalesce in apocalyptic expectation, both in general and in specific texts like the hymn from the Dead Sea Scrolls quoted earlier; they coalesce also in the New Testament proclamation. As is well known, before the exile there was no positive view of the after-life, and in most of the Old Testament man is described as mortal, bound to dissolve in death; man came from the dust, and to dust he will return, like the grass he fades away. If anything survives, it is just a shade of the person's former self, living in an underworld of ghosts and dreams, of darkness and forgetfulness. There there is no praise of God – it is a land of silence. The thought of Sheol always produced feelings of hopelessness. Hope lay in escape from Sheol, and for this, moving prayers were offered for healing, or victory. At least in this sense, of preventing death, God was seen as more powerful than the grave; but there was, generally speaking, no ultimate hope. Yet in Israel's faith, hope in God was never entirely absent. The prophets foresaw revival for the nation after judgment:

Come let us return to the Lord;
for he has torn that he may heal us;
he has stricken, and he will bind us up.
After two days he will revive us;
on the third day he will raise us up,
that we may live before him (Hos. 6.1-2).

Ezekiel described this revival in terms of a new creative act –
a new breathing of life into bones dry as dust:

Thus says the Lord God to these bones:
Behold I will cause breath to enter you, and you shall live.
And I will lay sinews upon you, and will cause flesh to come
upon you and cover you with skin, and put breath in you,
and you shall live; and you shall know that I am the Lord
(Ezek. 37.5–6).

Thus says the Lord God:
Behold I will open your graves, and raise you from your
graves, O my people; and I will bring you home to the land
of Israel. And you shall know that I am the Lord, when I
open your graves, and raise you from your graves, O my people
(Ezek. 37.12–13).

Ezekiel spoke of the nation's restoration in history; yet here
were the seeds of a doctrine of resurrection – the individual's
resurrection to new life, and the creation's resurrection to new
perfection and fulfilment. So in the Isaiah Apocalypse, our
symbol of judgment, the image of the travailing woman who
cannot successfully deliver, is juxtaposed with the hope of
resurrection:

Thy dead shall live, their bodies shall rise.
O dwellers in the dust, awake and sing for joy (Isa. 26.19).

Death and resurrection, travail and deliverance, despair and
hope – these form a persistent pattern in the prophetic and
apocalyptic tradition, and they provide the context of the New
Testament proclamation.

* * *

What then are we to make of all this? It is one thing to observe the dynamics of thought in an ancient text. It is another thing to make sense of them in a way that we can appropriate in a differing age and culture. It is not easy for us to recreate the situation of the early Christians. There has, after all, been a two-thousand-year delay in the fulfilment of their hopes for the future, and this rather takes the sense of cataclysm out of our range of thinking – not to mention the fact that our understanding of the structure of the universe excludes the possibility of taking predictions of the Second Coming at their face-value. True, the possibility of a nuclear holocaust has led to a kind of popular apocalypticism, and the influence of Marxism has led to a rediscovery of the *future* perspective inherent in early Christian eschatology and attempts to reaffirm it in more modern dress.[5] Yet as a serious proposal for coherent theology, the categories of apocalyptic do not appear very promising. They are too tied to artificial schemata of history, to mythological dramas of cosmic conflict, to primitive cosmology and strange visionary experiences.

However, I am increasingly sure that this sense of hope in the midst of despair, courage in the face of torment, confidence that in spite of all the odds God will make things right, is so central to the New Testament faith that we miss the heart of the Christian message if we cannot find a way of doing justice to it. Furthermore, I think that our puzzlement over the doctrine of atonement can be alleviated if we insist that this is the context in which the key texts have to be interpreted.

Without necessarily feeling obliged to appropriate all the apocalyptic dressing (and the New Testament itself to a very large extent avoids it, eschewing detailed apocalyptic timetables even while adopting its images), I find that there are two aspects of apocalyptic thinking that are entirely realistic. The first is its acceptance that the present state of the world is far from satisfactory. The second is its confidence that nevertheless it is all under God and God's purposes will be worked out. Atonement is to do with making that hope credible. It may be impossible to appropriate the time-scale of apocalyptic, but we can appreciate the reality of the world's anguish, and the possibility of hope within it. Surely we can even grasp something of what it would mean to experience in anticipation the integration of all things into the creative purpose of God. The mythological dualism of apocalyptic is not acceptable – so much we admitted in the last chapter – yet we also agreed that we are now deeply conscious of what we may call the 'demonic' element in creation, in history, in ourselves. This awareness is often best highlighted in literature. Let me refer again to Asher Lev, the Hasidic artist driven to paint a crucifix. Right at the end of the book he faces banishment from his home and his community:

'Asher Lev,' the Rebbe said softly, 'You have crossed a boundary. I cannot help you. You are alone now. I give you my blessings.'

I came out of the Rebbe's office and walked past Rev Dorochoff's angry gaze and out of the building. I walked for hours then beneath the naked trees of the parkway along streets that had once been my world but were now cold and gone from me . . . Asher Lev, Hasid. Asher Lev, painter. I looked at my right hand, the hand with which I painted. There was power in that hand. Power to create and destroy. Power to bring pleasure and pain. Power to amuse and horrify. There was in that hand the demonic and the divine at one and the same time. The demonic and the divine were two aspects of the same force. Creation was demonic and divine. Creativity was demonic and divine. Art was demonic and divine . . . I was demonic and divine. Asher Lev, son of Aryeh and Rivkeh Lev, was the child of the Master of the Universe *and* the Other Side. Asher Lev paints good pictures and hurts people he loves. Then be a great painter, Asher Lev; that will be the only justification for all the pain you will cause. But as a great painter I will cause pain again if I must. Then become a greater painter. But I will cause pain again. Then become a still greater painter. Master of the Universe, will I live this way all the rest of my life? Yes, came the whisper from the branches of the trees. Now journey with me, my Asher.

Paint the anguish of all the world. Let people see the pain . . .
We must give a balance to the universe.[6]

Giving a balance to the universe – is that a clue to the dynamic
of atonement? Is atonement to do with the integration of all
things into the creative purposes of God? Could it be that the
cross is best understood as God taking responsibility for the
demonic element – God bearing the consequences of his act of
creation? For in the last analysis only God can be responsible
for producing a world like this, where pain and evil and sin are
constituents of the created order.

In the Old Testament there was awareness of this:

> I am the Lord and there is no other. I form light and create
> darkness. I make weal and create woe. I am the Lord who does
> all these things (Isa. 45.6–7).

Maybe the exiled prophet spoke so strongly because of the
particular context in which he found himself; maybe the sole
responsibility of God for all things had to be asserted to counter
dualistic assumptions. Yet this was in fact deeply rooted in older
Israelite religion, and in the prophetic interpretation of Israel's
turbulent history. Disaster meant God's judgment:

> See now that I, even I, am he, and there is no god beside
>   me;
> I kill and I make alive;
> I wound and I heal;
> and there is none that can deliver out of my hand
> (Deut. 32.39).

It was later reflection on the appalling implications of saying
that God was responsible for all evil, especially innocent suffering, which led to Satan acquiring such a prominent role in the
explanation of evil; the devil was necessary to avoid turning God
into a demon. Yet Satan resolves nothing. If God is God, and
only God is God, he must ultimately be responsible for the
existence and character of Satan – as indeed the book of Job
recognizes. So, to repeat, in the last analysis, God alone can be

responsible for producing a world like this, and this being so, it may be that the most fruitful way of understanding the cross is in relation to theodicy, to see it as a way of justifying the ways of God by exposing the fact that he himself is at work in the suffering and agony of the world he created, labouring to produce a new creation. In the biblical tradition, it is Israel or the creation which suffers in travail rather than God. Yet once the cry of the labouring woman was ascribed to God, and maybe in Christ we may discern an implicit extension of the image, the implicit correlation of the threads we have traced – God involved in creation's labour-pains, God actively bearing the brunt of the pain, God submitting to judgment and taking punishment. So perhaps we might dare to suggest that God suffers the birth-pangs of his people, that God takes responsibility for the appalling consequences of his act of creation.

It was Simone Weil who perceived particularly clearly the cost to God of his act of creation:

The Creation is an abandonment. In creating what is other than himself, God necessarily abandoned it . . .

Because he is the creator, God is not all-powerful. Creation is abdication. But he is all-powerful in this sense, that his abdication is voluntary. He knows its effects and wills them . . .

God has emptied himself. This means that both the Creation and the Incarnation are included with the Passion . . .

At the end of such meditations, one reaches an extremely simple view of the universe. God has created, that is, not that he has produced something outside himself, but that he has withdrawn himself, permitting a part of being to be other than God . . .

The apparent absence of God in this world is the actual reality of God.[7]

God's creative love which maintains us in existence is not merely a superabundance of generosity, it is also renunciation and sacrifice. Not only the Passion but the Creation itself is a renunciation and sacrifice on the part of God . . . God already voids himself of his divinity by the Creation . . . His love maintains in existence, in a free and autonomous existence, beings other than himself, beings other than the good, mediocre beings. Through love he abandons them to affliction and sin. For if he did not abandon them they would not exist. His presence would annul their existence as a flame kills a butterfly . . .

It is by an inconceivable love that he comes down so far as to reach them . . . The Passion is not separable from the Creation. The Creation itself is a kind of passion. My very existence is like a laceration of God, a laceration which is love . . . The evil which we see everywhere in the world in the form of affliction and crime is a sign of the distance between us and God. But this distance is love, and therefore it should be loved.[8]

It has often been argued that to give creatures freewill is to risk sin, that to provide a consistent environment is to risk hurt, that moral education requires a world like this. To a large extent that is true, but even so it is not an all-embracing and satisfactory justification of the presence of evil, sin and suffering in the world. It simply does not take the matter seriously enough. Perhaps the insight of Simone Weil helps us to probe further. The very act of creation implied the withdrawal of God. The very act of loving implied forsaking, allowing independence, permitting the demonic. If that is so, then the act of atonement is to be found in God himself bearing the painful consequences of his own act of creative love. The creation has a negative aspect, an independence of God which inevitably brings with it a kind of 'futility', a built-in judgment, an 'existential estrangement'. Atonement means the transformation of this situation by God himself; it means, in Tillich's terms, God's participation in existential estrangement and its self-destructive consequences;[9] it means God submitting to the judgment, to the pain and the travail, so that by means of the labour a new world may be born.

Perhaps, then, we should understand the cross as indeed a symbol of all the pain that ever was, but more than a symbol – a

58

kind of gathering up of all pain, a reservoir of all pain, which becomes God's way of sharing the agony and ecstasy of his creation. The reality of the situation is not ignored, nor is it given a mere cosmetic dressing; it is affirmed and entered into, so that the integration of the agony and the ecstasy can be effected.

Seen like this, the gospel of Christ is what gives us the power to live in tension with sin and evil – in the world, in ourselves – but with hope, not despair. We can both be utterly realistic about it all, and yet transcend it. One of the most remarkable books I have read is *Dying we Live*,[10] a collection of letters which is subtitled: The final messages and records of some Germans who defied Hitler. The letters ring with hope and joy in the midst of cruelty and certain death. Paul Schneider wrote to his wife:

> Whatever happens to us now, dearest, rest assured that I bear your suffering too. But let us both rest assured of this, that the Lord Jesus and the faithful father heart of God have themselves before this borne our pain, and therefore he cannot let us be tried beyond our strength, but will see to it that the trial comes to such an end that we can bear it.

Ewald von Kleist-Schmenzin writes from prison:

> Precious beyond all else are the love and mercy of God who will save everyone who believes in him from all distress and all pain, and who even in this earthly life gives help through his Spirit. God has revealed to us everything that we need for living and dying. I have actually experienced it: 'Nevertheless I am continually with thee. Thou has holden me by thy right hand . . .' In his loving-kindness he has drawn me to himself again.

Ludwig Steil writes:

> The hymns of praise that come from those who live in need and misery are certainly more beautiful than those of the angels who never walked in the 'valley of shadow' . . . You cannot imagine what an advantage we Christians have in

prison over those who have no hope. Some of them are brave, but somehow still despairingly sad.

A cabin boy, Kim, tells of his feelings after torture:

> an exultant intoxication of victory, a joy so irrational that I was as though paralysed . . . it was as if the jubilation of the whole world had been gathered together here . . . Immediately afterwards it dawned upon me that I have now a new understanding of the figure of Jesus . . . I will warrant that the suffering endured in having a few nails driven through one's hands, in being crucified, is something purely mechanical that lifts the soul into an ecstasy comparable with nothing else.
>
> Since then I have often thought of Jesus. I can well understand the measureless love he felt for all men, and especially for those who took part in driving the nails into his hands . . . Jesus felt how his whole life was burning itself out of his own fiery force in a last concentration of everything that was strongest in him.

 Yes, the gospel of Christ is what gives us the power to live in tension with sin and evil; but with hope, not despair. Now this kind of approach to the doctrine of atonement actually takes up the essential core of each of the theories explored in the last chapter, and furthermore it meets their inadequacies. In the first place it affirms that the atoning process originated from God, is an act of *God's initiative* for the salvation of his people. Yet at the same time, it does not turn a blind eye to the ghastly fact of estrangement and sin. It is not mere sentimentality – it is a bearing of sin and guilt and shame, a costly sharing in the painful consequences of it all, a submission to judgment. There is no conflict between justice and love; for they are two sides of the same coin. Nor does it imply that the situation has simply been wafted away with a magic wand, that really it no longer exists. Rather, it proves that the situation, though real and continuing, can be transcended.

If this is a helpful analysis, it surely implies that atonement is no more and no less than the presence of God in the midst of all that denies him. I suggest that an important clue to this is to be found in the book of Job. This is the biblical book which wrestles most concentratedly with the problem of suffering. Yet commentators sometimes despair of the book – it poses all the problems and yet apparently gives no answer. The prose story which encapsulates the book (chapters 1 and 2, and 42.7ff.) is inconsistent with the poetic dialogues intervening: in the former, Job is submissive and never disloyal; in the latter, Job's patience cracks. In the dialogues Job never actually faces up to the comments of his comforters; rather, he presses his case against God, refusing to admit his guilt, demanding redress. Yet when God appears, all he does is to stun Job into silence – he offers no solution, no justification, nothing relevant to Job's protests. What, then, is the conclusion of the debate? Perhaps we can get to the bottom of it more effectively if we direct our attention away from the problem of innocent suffering to another aspect of the text. Suppose the heart of the problem for the Job of the dialogues is how to reach God. Several times Job demands a confrontation with God; for only if God gives the verdict can his innocence be proved. If he could put his case to God, he is sure God will defend him. But as long as he cannot reach God, that assurance is in doubt; God seems to be a law unto himself, to be quite arbitrary in his dealings with men, even malicious. How is Job to understand him? In Job's speeches it is the *absence* of God which is most painfully felt. So perhaps the solution to the interpretative puzzle is this: that the fact of God's presence satisfies Job rather than what he says. When God himself appears, no explanations are necessary. In his presence, anything and everything is bearable. The only proper response is humble acceptance. For Job, and indeed for the prophet Isaiah (6.1–8), confrontation with the presence of God was a humbling and a purging experience. As Rudolf Otto[11] discerned, being in the presence of the Holy One effects atonement in itself. For that experience is a paradoxical one: on the one hand, it is an overwhelming sense of unworthiness, of creatureliness, of being polluted and needing to hide; on the other hand, it is a profound sense of purging and renewal, of gracious acceptance, of consecration. Atonement is effected by the very presence of God.

The proclamation of Jesus was that the kingdom of God was imminent – indeed, breaking in already. In his parables and his actions, he demonstrated the reality of God's coming, and God's power over evil and sin. By his presence people seemed to face divine judgment. In his life, in his death, in his resurrection, people were confronted with the presence of God in the midst of everything that seemed opposed to his rule. Of course such statements raise the further question, what do we mean by speaking of the presence of God in the man Jesus; but that is not the immediate issue here.[12] It merely goes to show that all questions of Christian theology are interrelated. The point here is that the early Christians discerned in Jesus the fulfilment of all God's promises, the beginning of the End-time, *the coming of God*. So it was that they lived in hope and confidence and joy and expectation, even in the midst of dire trials and tribulations. They were convinced that God was present in their midst; for in Jesus and through the Spirit, the final confrontation with God was anticipated. The presence of God meant that they could stand the fires of judgment, survive the final woes, and emerge refined and purified in God's new world. The very chapter in Romans that uses the image of the travailing woman culminates in the following cry of triumph:

> What then shall we say on top of this? If God is on our side, who is against us? After all, it was God who did not spare his own Son, but gave him up for us all; so how could he not shower us with all blessings along with him? Who is there to bring charges against the elect of God? For God is the one who does the acquitting. Who is there to condemn? Christ Jesus who died and was risen, who is at the right-hand of God, who intercedes on our behalf? What can separate us from the love of Christ? Tribulation or distress or persecution or hunger or nakedness or danger or sword? . . . No. In all these things we are winning an overwhelming victory through him who loved us. I am persuaded that neither death nor life,

neither angels nor princes, neither things present nor things to come, neither powers nor height nor depth, nor any other created thing will be able to separate us from the love of God which is in Christ Jesus our Lord (Rom. 8.31–9; my translation).

When Trevor Huddleston wrote his foreword to *Dying we Live*, he picked out one telling sentence: 'God has become more real and more immediate to me.' Yet, he comments, these people 'were living in the shadow of death: and they were living with that which should, humanly speaking, have produced a dread and a despair in the soul. For nothing, I suppose, in the long history of human cruelty, has exceeded the Nazi concentration camps and the vile philosophy of life which produced them.' 'God has become more real and immediate to me.' That is their triumphant message in the midst of the horror of human sin, suffering and demonic evil. The presence of God effects atonement, because it brings hope and joy and peace – the possibility of new inner freedom, the possibility of redeeming the situation, of 'giving a balance to the universe'.

So the gospel-message is essentially simple. It is the proclamation that in spite of appearances, God is in it all with us. That is the basis of Christian hope. It is the reality of atonement – at-one-ment being the integration of the deep tensions built into God's world, an integration effected through the reality of God's presence.

4

The Wedding Feast

We thank you, Lord, that you have fed us in this sacrament,
united us with Christ, and given us a foretaste of the heavenly
banquet prepared for all mankind.

The Methodist Service-Book

In the previous chapter I suggested that, in spite of all the
difficulties, it was only in the overall context of apocalyptic
thinking that biblical material concerning atonement could be
adequately grasped. It is in the light of that kind of perspective
that specific controversial texts have to be re-examined. To that
task we now turn. As indicated previously, the problems cluster
about the true meaning in the New Testament of 'propitiation',
'redemption', 'reconciliation' and 'justification', and the role of
the 'blood of Christ' in bringing these conditions into being.
Now these terms come from different contexts, from the jargon
of the law-courts and the battlefield, the social institution of
slavery and the religious practice of sacrifice. The first two are
still with us, the last two are not. Some of the controversy over
meaning arises precisely because language is used in the New
Testament which has since 'gone dead' – it no longer makes
direct reference to living conventions. As in the case of apocalyptic, we have to make some effort of study and imagination to
project ourselves back into a situation where such language *was*

meaningful, and so come to grips with all its resonances and potential.

Clearly the language of sacrifice is crucial. The significance of blood in sacrifice, whatever that significance was, must have furnished the basic material which allowed the blood of Christ to strike chords in people's minds. In the fully developed law accepted in New Testament times as the gift of God to his people, sacrifice was primarily associated with the need to do something about sin. The early Christians proclaimed that Christ died for our sins, that Christ Jesus was a *hilastērion* through faith in his blood. Precisely how such expressions are to be interpreted lies at the heart of the liberal-conservative controversy. The conservative understands them to mean that Christ's blood was shed in payment of the penalty properly exacted for our sin by God's righteousness, to propitiate the entirely justifiable wrath of God at our sinfulness, and so reconcile us to the Holy One we had offended. This interpretation correlates the sacrificial language with that of redemption, justification and reconciliation, seeing them all referring to aspects of the one act which was necessary to obtain God's forgiveness without compromising his justice. The liberal wants to give a very different exegesis, emphasizing the love and mercy of God rather than his wrath and judgment. The question is whether either interpretation does justice to the text. Let us survey the debate and consider the strengths and weaknesses on each side, concentrating on the most contentious text, Romans 3.25a: '(Jesus Christ) whom God put forward as a *hilastērion* through faith in his blood.' To do this we must submit ourselves for a while to disciplined and exact study of precise details so that we may assess adequately crucial points in the argument.

C. H. Dodd in his commentary on Romans[1] refers at this point (on 3.25) to his article on 'atonement' in *The Bible and the Greeks*,[2] and it is worth following it up. There he examines the use of words related to *hilastērion* in the Septuagint (the Greek version of the Old Testament), and though admitting that in classical Greek the usual rendering must be 'propitiation', basically argues that in the Bible, the meaning is 'expiation'. The difference here is that 'propitiation' implies placation, averting the anger of a deity, whereas 'expiation' implies purgation, getting rid of sin. The first can be interpreted in accordance with the Anselmian theory, the second need not carry the same implications.

To establish his case Dodd uses a linguistic method which depends on the fact that words in different languages do not exactly correspond with one another, and a translator may well vary the way he renders a word into another language. These variations will give clues as to what the translator thought were synonyms, and so his basic conception of the kind of meaning particular words carried may be discerned. So Dodd here examines the words other than *hilaskesthai* (the verb from which *hilastērion* is derived) used by the Septuagint translators for the Hebrew word *kipper* (usually translated into English as 'to make atonement'). They render it, he says, by words which give the meaning 'to sanctify' or 'to purify' persons or ritual objects, or 'to cancel', 'to purge away' or 'to forgive' sins. We should therefore expect to find that they regard the class of words we are interested in as conveying similar ideas. Dodd then examines the Hebrew words other than *kipper* which are translated by *hilaskesthai*, etc., and concludes that they are used in one of two senses: with a human subject, they mean 'to cleanse from sin or defilement', that is, 'to expiate'; with a divine subject, they mean 'to be gracious', 'to have mercy', 'to forgive'. Where these words render *kipper*, he then suggests, they carry the same kind of connotations; so the Septuagint translators did not regard *kipper* as conveying the sense of propitiating the deity but the sense of performing an act whereby guilt or defilement is removed. When he turns to the New Testament passages where such words are used, he is equipped with these findings, and they are confirmed. In Hebrews 2.17, for example, *sins* appear as the *object* of the verb. So the meaning in the Bible must be 'expiate', not 'propitiate' as in pagan Greek. Dodd explains this development of sense by reference to the overall moral and theological context of the Bible: because God alone could annul defilement, the verb came to be used with God as subject in the sense 'to forgive'. So the noun *hilastērion* which appears in Romans 3.25 must mean 'a means by which guilt is annulled or sin purged'. In this text the subject is God: God produces the *hilastērion*. So it can hardly mean 'propitiation' or 'placation', which implies something done to God; it must mean that God provides the means whereby the guilt of sin is removed, by sending Christ. Christ is the divine method of forgiveness. Such is the 'liberal' approach to the exegesis of this text.

In his book *The Apostolic Preaching of the Cross*,[3] Leon Morris sets out the opposite view. If the Septuagint translators and the New Testament writers did *not* mean propitiation, why did they choose to use words which signify propitiation and are saturated with propitiatory associations? Morris criticizes Dodd's method: it is only capable of giving the meaning of the word-group in a very general way, and is linguistically unsound given the wide range of meanings a word may have in any given language. He also questions Dodd's statistics, and suggests that his claims concerning usage in the Septuagint are exaggerated. In Hebrews 2.17, it is likely that the accusative is an 'accusative of respect' rather than the direct object: so the text should be translated 'to make propitiation *with regard to* the sins of the people'. Not all the detailed points Morris makes are convincing, but most compelling is his discussion of the *context* in which words are used. The context in Romans is a long description of the 'wrath of God' and its consequences; the context in the Old Testament is divine judgment on the sins of Israel. Given this context, 'propitiation' is the more natural meaning of these words, in the Bible as in pagan Greek.

Now in his commentary, Dodd makes no attempt to link up his view of the wrath of God with his interpretation of *hilastērion*; but clearly, as Morris observed, there is a close connection. Dodd had already argued in his commentary that God is not angry in a crude anthropomorphic sense. Paul never uses the verb 'to be angry' with God as subject. He only refers to the wrath as the wrath *of God* three times. The wrath is actually used in an impersonal sort of way. What Paul means, Dodd claims, is a process of cause and effect built into the universe:

sin is the cause, disaster the effect. Wrath has come to mean in Paul, not an *attitude* of God to man, but an inevitable process within a moral universe.

Leon Morris tackles this view of the wrath of God. He admits that the biblical writers have nothing to do with pagan conceptions of a capricious and vindictive deity inflicting arbitrary punishments on offending worshippers who must then bribe him back to a good mood by appropriate offerings. Yet for him to demonstrate how real and serious the wrath of God is in the Old Testament hardly posed any problem. In the Bible, he notes, God may not be capriciously angry, but he is a moral being, and he is consistent in his demands. There is a stern reaction of the divine nature to evil in man, and it is caused only and inevitably by sin. Morris points to the biblical insistence on the sovereignty of God. Punishment comes from him as much as forgiveness. It is hard to imagine how the prophets and psalmists could possibly have expressed more strongly the personal aspect of the wrath of God. Mercy is the action of the same God who 'allows his wrath to be turned away' (Micah 8.18, Ps. 85, 2ff.); God is 'slow to anger' and 'plentiful in mercy'. But the destruction of Jerusalem was God's doing, and this is deeply engrained in the prophetic interpretation of history.

Leon Morris then argued that the removal of wrath is definitely in view when words like *hilaskesthai* are used. Where there is sin, there is wrath. Forgiveness involves the *turning aside of wrath*. In other words, some kind of satisfaction or payment to God's justice is required. Thus Leon Morris demonstrates that the Anselmian theory, or an objective view of atonement, is scriptural. Indeed, given the prominence of wrath and judgment in the first three chapters of Romans, he has no difficulty in arguing that *hilastērion* must mean a propitiatory action whereby the wrath of God is averted and men brought into a new relationship with God.

Now careful examination of the issues involved, and the arguments employed in the course of this dispute, suggests to me that there is some substance in what both sides say. Leon Morris is right to draw attention to the wrath and judgment of God as the biblical context in which these words are used: and it is certain that Greek-speaking converts are likely to have understood the word *hilastērion* in terms of propitiation – indeed, for the most part, the Greek Fathers of the church accepted that exegesis without question. Yet Dodd also makes an important point: we have to take account of the fact that language was modified when torn from its pagan roots and used in the context of Israel's religion. Justice has to be done to the fact that God does not generally appear in the Bible as the recipient of a placatory offering or as the object of an atoning action – indeed, he is often explicitly the *subject*, as he is in the very sentence in Romans 3.25 which we have been examining. Leviticus 17.11 implies that God gave the people the blood as a means of atonement, as Leon Morris himself admits. The people did not offer bribes to buy off God's anger; indeed, the prophets condemned those who thought they could get away with that kind of thing. Rather, God in his mercy provided the sacrificial system for his people, so that sin could be dealt with and the covenant kept in being. In the time of the New Testament, it seems to have been generally assumed that the sacrifices were to be offered simply *because God commanded them*, and the Epistle to the Hebrews suggests that their purpose was regarded as purificatory and nothing else (Heb. 9.22). The Greek Fathers were not insensitive to this point either, although most of them did not integrate it systematically with their understanding of *hilaskesthai* as propitiation. There is some substance in what both sides say. So how are we to resolve this interpretative problem?

Suppose we reconsider the whole discussion in the light of the previous chapter. It should be clear that 'the wrath of God' was not understood by Paul as 'an inevitable process of cause and effect built into the universe'; nor was it a personal reaction of God to the sins of individuals. Rather, it meant the eschatological woes, the great cataclysm of agony, destruction and disaster which had begun to afflict the creation, including Gentiles as well as Jews, a cataclysm which would nevertheless be the 'birth-pangs' of the new age. These woes were an expression of God's judgment on everything that had gone wrong with his creation.

The question was how would anyone survive. One could escape only if one could survive the judgment. One could survive the judgment only if sin had been dealt with and so a favourable verdict in the final court (i.e. justification) was obtainable. What Israel had learned in the course of her history was that in the final analysis God alone could rescue the people from judgment; that God alone could save; that through the fires of judgment, God himself purged the people of their sins, and in his mercy provided a system for on-going purification and sanctification. Repentance and obedience to the law were the only demands God made of his people, but obedience to the law included the performance of sacrifice, the cultic use of blood to keep everything holy: 'For the life of the flesh is in the blood, and I have given it for you upon the altar to make atonement for your souls; for it is the blood that makes atonement by reason of the life' (Lev. 17.11). For Paul it was self-evident that the sins of the old order had to be dealt with before the new order could come to birth. So God provided the ultimate means of atonement which fulfilled and abrogated every previous provision – it was the final expiation, the sacrificial blood of Jesus Christ. Those who accepted this gracious gift of God's mercy would be enabled to survive the fires of wrath, would find themselves acquitted at the last great assize, and would be reborn or resurrected in the promised new world. This kind of understanding is even more evident in the Epistle to the Hebrews. There the sacrifice of Christ is final in the literal sense that it belongs to the final act of winding up the old order and bringing in the new. It was the only perfectly adequate sin-offering, but it was also the seal of the covenant-bond. It was axiomatic that blood was needed to purify, and that blood was needed to seal a covenant. No one would think of questioning the assumptions built into the old law. But seeing the death of Christ as the fulfilment of the old law meant an entirely new perspective. It was God's way of making his creatures fit to survive the final judgment and be received into the heavenly Jerusalem purged and renewed. Thus one way of dealing with the dispute over interpretation is to put the texts in a different overall perspective by examining them in the light of an appropriate understanding of their background – namely the apocalyptic outlook discussed in the last chapter.

But even so, I wonder if we have really got to the bottom of this sacrificial language. Could it not be that the terms of the debate about atonement have been too constricting? Have we assumed too quickly that sacrifice is exclusively concerned with the problem of sin? Have we been in too much of a hurry to relate it to the theme of justification? I am afraid we have. Indeed, I am convinced that the whole notion of sacrifice has become seriously distorted because we focus too exclusively on these controversial texts and interpret them in the light of uncriticized assumptions about the nature and purpose of sacrifice. Not only has the notion been distorted by these debates over atonement, but also by the controversies at the Reformation about the sacrifice of the Mass, and by contemporary usage of the word in a culture which no longer practises and therefore no longer instinctively understands what it is all about. Popular usage suggests that the nub of sacrifice lies in giving up something. Unenlightened theological usage suggests that sacrifice is some kind of compensation for sin. The two come together in the practice of giving up sweets for Lent. This is an entirely inadequate understanding which misses altogether the resonances and associations originally implicit in the material.[4]

We need look no further than another text in Romans to get a clue to the wider meaning of sacrifice:

> I appeal to you brethren to present your bodies as a living sacrifice, holy and acceptable to God, which is your spiritual worship (Rom. 12.1).

The definition of sacrifice is there in the text: sacrifice is worship and worship is sacrifice. In the world in which the church grew up, religion without sacrifice was unthinkable – indeed, since the Christians did not practise sacrifice, they rapidly became known as atheists. Inevitably they picked up the religious language of their contemporaries – indeed, the language of the Old Testament was formative in their understanding of the gospel they had to proclaim. So they spoke of sacrifice. But to grasp the significance of this, it is essential to re-enter their world, to realize how central sacrifice was to all religion.

Now the best approach to understanding the idea of sacrifice is to think of reasons why you give presents or throw a party. When you give a present, do you 'make a sacrifice' in the colloquial sense? If so, it is a shabby gift given with a poor grace! On the other hand, the gift has little value if it has cost you nothing in time, effort or expense. Similarly, a sacrifice had to represent some degree of self-denial, while at the same time being given in a willing, even loving and grateful spirit. You throw a party (which also costs something!) because you want to celebrate – a birthday, an engagement, a wedding; some sacrifices were festive occasions of that kind, annual celebrations, or more frequent fellowship-meals at which the deity was present. You give presents for the same kind of reasons, or perhaps as a way of saying 'thank you' or apologizing, making amends for something you have done, or as a way of asking a favour. Gifts and sacrifices, in a similar way, accompanied and reinforced prayers. So there were many different motives at work, many different rituals prescribed, depending on what it was you wished to do in your prayers or your worship. So in both pagan religion and the Old Testament, there were many types of sacrifice, expressing different things. There were communion-sacrifices in which the worshippers joined in a meal, offering parts of the sacrificial victim to the deity and enjoying the rest. There were offerings of praise and thanksgiving, gifts presented in homage; in the Old Testament, the holocausts or whole-burnt-offerings expressed this, symbolizing the gift of everything to God in gratitude. Then there were sin-offerings, offerings to make amends for, or get rid of sin, the faults which spoiled the relationship between God and his worshippers. In the Old Testament, increasing preoccupation with sin, particularly when the lesson of exile had been learned, led to a tendency to treat all sacrifices as ways of dealing with sin, and elaborate blood-rituals were prescribed on every occasion; but the other motivations persisted – as is clear from Paul's words in Romans 12.1, the starting point of our discussion. Sacrifice the use of the animal victims as well as other gifts in kind, was the standard and unquestioned method of facilitating communication with the divine, of worshipping; and in the Old Testament, besides these different types of 'regular' sacrifices, there were stories of special sacrifices cementing covenant-bonds with God (Abraham and God, Moses and God), as well as rather special quasi-sacrificial rituals associated with the annual celebration of Passover and the Day of Atonement.

There are two sides to worship; there is the spontaneous joyous response to God, the one who has done so much for his worshippers, and there is also the sense of obligation – worship should be offered, whether one feels like it or not, because God is God. Now clearly both these attitudes lay behind the performance of sacrifice, and in so far as for the Jews it was a fulfilling of the law required by God, the second tended to predominate; sacrifice became a duty performed as an obligation, especially as these cultic acts were concentrated in the Temple at Jerusalem and confined to the priests who followed a strict rota in their effort to fulfil every detail laid down in the Holy Torah. Yet in the Old Testament itself, spontaneous joy in worship is often depicted, and it is clearly expressed in the psalms. Both joy and obligation were expressed in synagogue worship, where 'spiritual sacrifices' replaced the literal fulfilment of the cult. At the time of the New Testament, the spiritualization of sacrifice in Judaism was well-advanced. In Ben Sira's work, the righteous man makes an offering by keeping the law; almsgiving is a sacrifice of thanksgiving; atonement may be effected by repentence and abstention from wickedness (Ecclus. 35.1–10). In the Dead Sea Scrolls we meet a sect that had rejected the current Temple practice as corrupt; instead they found spiritual ways of worship:

> They shall atone for guilty rebellion and for the sins of unfaithfulness that they may obtain loving-kindness for the land, without the flesh of holocausts and the fat of sacrifice. And prayer rightly offered shall be an acceptable fragrance of

righteousness and perfection of way, a delectable freewill offering.

Prayer was regarded as an 'offering of the lips', and righteous living was treated as capable of procuring God's favour and atonement.[5] Such ideas became the basis of Philo's allegorical understanding of sacrifices as symbols of the offering of spiritual and moral virtues. God does not rejoice in sacrifices, he affirmed, for all things are in his possession, and because he possesses all things, he is in need of none. Justice is more important than sacrifice; prayer is the highest form of worship. 'God rejoices in altars without fires around which virtues dance.' It is impossible to give God anything but praise.[6] The Rabbis, too, found alternatives to sacrifice, especially after the Fall of Jerusalem in AD 70 and the cessation of the cult. When Rabbi Joshua lamented, 'Woe to us, for the place wherein the sins of Israel were expiated is destroyed,' Rabbi Johanan ben Zakkai replied, 'We still have a means of expiation of equal value – the practice of kindness; for it is said, "I will have kindness not offering".'[7]

Now if we look at the New Testament with all this in mind, we soon find a much richer use of sacrificial ideas than is at first apparent. As Paul indicated in Romans 12.1, Christians adopted these widespread spiritualizing ideas: to dedicate one's life to God was the ultimate in sacrifice, and the proper offering of worship. It was both joy and obligation – it had consequences for one's life-style. Christians were enjoined to be holy and faultless in a moral sense, just as the sacrificial victims had been physically pure and without blemish according to the law (Phil. 2.15–17; but see also the context of Rom. 12.1). This kind of dedication was a response of praise and thanksgiving, just like the holocausts or whole-burnt offerings of the old law. This is more explicit in the Epistle to the Hebrews when (echoing the Dead Sea Scrolls) it speaks of a sacrifice of praise, the fruit of lips which confess his name (13.15); and then in the following verse describes doing good and sharing as sacrifices well-pleasing to God. This is not the only place where acts of charity are spoken of in sacrificial terms: the financial help sent to Paul by the Philippians he describes as an *osmē euodias* (using the Old Testament phrase a 'sweet savour'), a sacrifice acceptable and well-pleasing to God (Phil. 4.18). People had long since abandoned the idea that God actually got pleasure from the taste or smell of the burning flesh on the altar; but the language remained fossilized, and wherever the word *osmē*, fragrance, appears, it brings with it the connotations of sacrifices God is pleased to accept. For Paul, Christians by their worship and their lives, released a kind of incense into the atmosphere, an incense which could attract or repel others, bringing about their salvation or condemnation (II Cor. 2.14–16). Furthermore, communion with the Lord meant table-fellowship with him, sharing his life, receiving his vitality: that is why you could not have it both ways and communicate with demons as well by participating in pagan revelries (I Cor. 10.16–22). Such ideas derived their force from contemporary assumptions about what happened in sacrifice. So through using sacrificial language, Paul conveys the idea that God and his worshippers take pleasure in each other, and that accounts for the fact that there is so much rejoicing in the Pauline letters.

Now what difference does it make to look at the sacrifice of Christ in this much wider context? I think it is clear that the early Christians did not associate it only with sin-offerings. The death of Christ was for them the perfect offering of homage, loyalty and obedience to God, as well as the perfect answer to sin. That is how it could be seen as the way of cementing a new relationship between God and the world. When Christians spoke of the sacrificial death of Christ, they saw it as the fulfilment and consummation of everything that the Old Testament had understood to be the God-given means of uniting God and his people in covenant with one another. St Augustine, one of the great Fathers of the church, wrote: "True sacrifice is every act designed to unite us to God in holy fellowship."[8]

The uniting of God with us in fellowship comes through worship, and what the Christian tradition says is that the sacrifice of Christ on the cross is the means whereby that uniting is made possible.

That this kind of understanding did lie at the heart of the New Testament use of sacrificial language is proven, it seems to me, by the Epistle to the Hebrews. I have suggested that there were many different types of sacrifice corresponding to the different things that worshippers wished to express; that these different kinds are all to be found in the Old Testament, along with special rituals for particular annual occasions like the Passover and the Day of Atonement; and that the sealing of the covenant-bond had been accomplished through sacrificial blood. Now what happens in the Epistle to the Hebrews is that all these different types of sacrifice are seen as fulfilled in Jesus' death. Features from one ritual after another appear in a hotch-potch as you work through chapters 9 and 10: the Day of Atonement rituals are fulfilled in Christ, so are the daily sin-offerings, and so are other special purificatory rites like those prescribed for a leper on the day of his cleansing (Heb. 9.19; cf. Lev. 14.4ff. for details which do not come from Ex. 24.6-8). The blood of the old rituals purified the flesh and the material cult-objects in the Temple; the blood of Christ, claims the Epistle, fulfils and surpasses, for it cleanses the conscience. Once for all purgation has been effected. Furthermore, the blood of Christ sealed the new covenant, fulfilling and abrogating the old established by Moses. All the imperfections and inadequacies of the old are dealt with, and an entirely new situation is created. And the whole conglomeration of ideas culminates in a crucial passage in chapter 10 where the author (whoever he was) quotes from Psalm 40:

> Sacrifices and offerings thou hast not desired,
> but a body hast thou prepared for me;
> In burnt-offerings and sin-offerings thou hast taken no pleasure.
> Then I said, 'Lo, I have come to do thy will, O God',
> as it is written of me in the roll of the book.

In the crucial second line of this quotation, the Hebrew original has a strange idiom, 'You have dug ears for me', which implies that the psalmist has been prepared to hear and respond to God's word, and closely parallels the phrase about doing

God's will in the succeeding verse. Yet the Epistle reads, 'You have furnished me with a body.' Clearly some textual confusion has arisen, and it must have arisen in the Greek version since the two words 'body' and 'ears' could only be confused in Greek. Yet what a providential slip on the part of that careless scribe! As the following verses of the Epistle indicate, it is precisely upon this error that the author of Hebrews is able to build the apex of his theology. His understanding is that the old prophetic criticisms of sacrifice were right; God does not want that kind of worship. What he wants is the complete dedication of obedience (Lo I have come to do thy will, O God); and in offering his body to death, Christ offered that supreme act of homage, that supreme sacrifice of praise, total self-offering. Before such a sacrifice all other sacrifices pale into insignificance: they are nothing worth, they are annulled and abolished. In this Epistle at least it is clear that when the Christians spoke of the sacrificial death of Christ, they saw it as the fulfilment and consummation of everything that the Old Testament had understood to be the God-given means of uniting God and his people in fellowship with one another.

Now if this is really the kind of thing sacrifice is all about, then all the various themes and ideas we have been exploring dove-tail together in a remarkably consistent way. Atonement it was suggested earlier, is the integration of the deep tensions built into God's world. Atonement is necessary because the very act of creation implies allowing the creation autonomy, it implies God abandoning his creation to be itself. Atonement is effected by God's presence in the midst of everything which denies him, everything which proclaims his absence. Now sacrifice, if it be the restoration of fellowship, the re-uniting of God with his creatures, if it be true worship, the declaration of God's praises and submission to his will, then it is at the very heart of the atoning process. The sacrifice of Christ was not a bribe to buy off God's anger, nor was it simply an expression of God's love for us. It was the mutual participation of God and man in a costly effort to reintegrate what had been torn asunder.

That reintegrating process involves us as well as God. In

both in JC, only one

principle Christ's sacrifice can be understood to contain the whole two-way process: God's self-emptying in renunciation and sacrifice so that his presence might be realized within his estranged creation, and man's sacrificial act of homage in obedience unto death. Yet the uniting of God and man in fellowship is not complete without our participation in it – the 'subjective' element is as important as the 'objective'. For our response of worship to be consummated, everything that gets in the way has to be dealt with, and that too, according to the New Testament, was accomplished by the sacrifice of Christ, the ultimate sin-offering.

What, then, gets in our way and how are we to conceive of these blockages being removed by the death of Christ? The traditional Western answer has always been that sin and the guilt of it is the fundamental blockage, and the various theories revolve around mechanisms for resolving this particular problem. It is necessary on our side to find release from guilt before we can be united with God. For some it has been sufficient that the love of God displayed in the sacrificial death of Jesus moved them to repentance; but in fact receiving forgiveness is often far harder than we imagine. We are all far too proud to receive forgiveness because we hate admitting we are wrong, and if we do admit it, we like to earn forgiveness by making amends. If we are to receive forgiveness, we either have to sense that we are purified, that somehow our sin has been blotted out and we really are acceptable (expiation); or we have to feel that some amends have been made for what we have done (propitiation). It is therefore a fact of experience that people respond to the sacrifice of Christ as a way of making amends on their behalf, or as a way of cleansing their faults. The old sacrificial system met the same kind of needs, one way or the other. God in his mercy provided the means whereby our sense of guilt is broken down, and we are released so that unity with God is made possible.

Another blockage is our wretched self-sufficiency, itself the deepest manifestation of sin, the fact that we want to do everything for ourselves. If we are going to reach a point in which we engage in genuine worship, we need to sense what it means to give up our own claims and just be grateful. We need to discover that thanksgiving is at the very root of our response to God. It is this which gives us the joy and the release and the unity with God which we are seeking. It is only when we get this sense that God has done for us what we could not do for ourselves, that this response becomes possible. This is one of the most important insights of the New Testament, phrased in different language – we are justified and sanctified *by faith alone*, by simply receiving in trust and not trying to do anything ourselves to rectify our position. Our pride does not like this: all our instincts are to maintain our autonomy. Yet when we are humbled by God's goodness and accept his grace, we discover that after all his service is perfect freedom. Sheer gratitude is an essential element in our participation in the atoning process. It breaks down our self-sufficiency.

But there are other things that get in the way of unity, and I suspect that the traditional theories have done us a disservice by concentrating too exclusively on sin and guilt and obscuring these other aspects. Perhaps the major blockage for many of us is our sense of the absence or callousness of God. So many people now doubt or deny God's existence, and the modern sciences have made it so plausible to believe that the universe is entirely autonomous. Besides, we are particularly conscious in this century of those things which make it hard to accept that the world was created by a good God: earthquakes and viruses, Auschwitz and Hiroshima. This aspect of atonement has already been explored a bit in the last chapter. The problem we have is Job's problem writ large; and Job's protests are our protests. We need the solution he was offered: a sense of the presence of God. No argument provides that; no religious experience is a knock-down proof; and dogmatic talk about incarnation can appear entirely implausible. Yet to the discerning eye of faith, stimulated by sensitive preaching or creative meditation, the man with arms outstretched on the cross can become a clue to the presence of God in the midst of all the world's tragedy. A God who takes responsibility for the awful mess that his creation has got into, even to the extent of sharing it, is one who has come to meet us even when least expected; our protests and doubts are silenced. The only appropriate response is to join in praise and worship.

Another problem is our frailty. We are not very good at recognizing this in the twentieth century, but the Eastern Orthodox tradition is very conscious of the distinction between the Creator and the creature, the sense that in order to approach the Creator, the frail creature has to bring some kind of offering, some kind of tribute, some adequate gift. If you go to the liturgy in any Orthodox church, you will find that what is expressed there is the church's re-presentation of the sacrifice of Christ – for man needs an offering to come into God's presence; and all we have is the offering put into our hands by God himself – the body and blood of our Lord.

In many and various ways, then, the sacrifice of Christ breaks down the barriers to true unity with God, and enables us to participate in fulfilment of our obligation in fitting worship, to offer the homage of total obedience and join in the heavenly banquet – the communion-sacrifice which unites all things to God in holy fellowship. Sacrifice is to do with worship, and it is the death of Christ which for the Christian tradition creates conditions in which it is possible for true worship to take place – for God and his people to be united in fellowship. Worship realizes the presence of God and the presence of God effects atonement. When man is in the presence of the holy, there is at the same time the profoundest sense of guilt, awe, fear and inadequacy, and the deepest sense of joy because the experience is itself a purging experience. Such was Rudolf Otto's insight, as we noticed earlier. This experience is at the heart of true worship. When we worship in the name of the one who gave himself for us, we are taken up into that purging and that joy.

But the joy over-rides everything. For, to put it in the eschatological terms of the New Testament, the death of Christ has finally dealt with all the problems of the old order, broken down all the barriers to proper realization of the covenant-relationship, and made it possible to join, at least in anticipation, in the feast of the kingdom. Have you noticed how often in the gospels the kingdom is likened to a wedding feast? Now to feast in the kingdom is to feast in God's presence, to rejoice in seeing him face to face; to feast in the kingdom is to worship him properly, to play one's part in the great congregation praising the God of our salvation, the multitude of every nation crying in a loud voice:

Salvation belongs to God who sits on the throne, and to the Lamb. Amen, blessing and glory and wisdom and thanksgiving and power and might be to our God for ever and ever (Rev. 7.10, 12).

Of course the final consummation has not yet been reached; yet the Christians of the New Testament experienced it in anticipation, and so might we. The old order is obsolescent, fading away; it still dogs our steps, but it cannot harm us. The pictures of the kingdom in the Bible are pictures of joy arising from the midst of affliction, joy arising from a people who had glimpsed a God who so loves that he shares in the darkness and the pain, comes to his people like a father and a shepherd, meets them on the way and lifts their burdens. They hope in God because God is the one who saves. They love and praise God in the midst of the pain and evil of the world. Even in the visions of the perfect future, the Lamb slain and the blood of the martyrs are at the centre of the praising congregation. All that is negative is embraced within the worship of God. So Christian worship no longer concentrates primarily on dealing with sin. Rather, the celebratory aspect of sacrifice is uppermost.

Let us continually offer up a sacrifice of praise to God, that is, the fruit of lips which acknowledge his name (Heb. 13.15).

Present your bodies as a living sacrifice, holy and acceptable to God, which is your spiritual worship . . . Rejoice in your hope, be patient in tribulation, be constant in prayer . . .
May the God of hope fill you with all joy and peace in believing so that by the power of the Holy Spirit you may abound in hope (Rom. 12.1,12; 15.3).

The New Testament, then, takes very seriously the fact that we belong to a good creation that has been corrupted; but it also rejoices in the beginning of its rebirth. The sacrifice of Christ is intimately involved in the necessary process of submitting to judgment and emerging from it triumphant, but for the believer there is nothing to do but accept and respond with sacrifices of praise and rejoicing because all has been accomplished by God in Christ. So the appropriate response is celebration and thanksgiving, and it is through worship of that kind that atonement is truly realized.

We thank you Lord that you have fed us in this sacrament, united us with Christ, and given us a foretaste of the heavenly banquet prepared for all mankind.

A Musical Interlude

The next few pages should not be regarded as a theology of music or anything else so grandiose. It is just an interlude, a pause for reflection, a few simple thoughts and tentative feelers after an appropriate and illuminating parable, a different way of grasping the truths we have been exploring. After all, analysis, however far it may serve us, is sometimes transcended by poetic insight, even if that insight needs to be tested and assessed through analytical thought; and words are not always the best vehicle for the deepest things we know, the things that have power to stir us. I have become more and more fascinated by the way in which music seems to be a parable of life, and it is through music that I have experienced most powerfully the integration of joy and sorrow, tragedy and hope.

Consider the second movement of Beethoven's Fourth Piano Concerto: a ruthless theme, asserted by the orchestra, is opposed to a plaintive melody on the piano, which gradually neutralizes the orchestra's opposition. Together the two ideas create the effect of a song of sorrow intermingled with violent sobbing protest, the fury of despair. The composer had recently seen a picture of Niobe, the tragic mother of Greek mythology, weeping over the death of her children; but it is likely that he was also expressing his own agony, that it is Beethoven's cry of despair at his incurable deafness. 'Beethoven did not write to please a small circle of connoisseurs, but to communicate to mankind a message which came from the very depth of his being; his music is the reply which his flesh and blood opposes to the repeated blows of fate.'[1] Beethoven himself prayed for the ability to escape his limitations, or at least transcend them. This was his prayer:

> O God give me strength to be victorious over myself, for nothing may chain me to this life. O guide my spirit, O raise me from these dark depths, that my soul, transported through Thy wisdom, may fearlessly struggle upward in fiery flight. For Thou alone understandest and canst inspire me.[2]

His music is itself the answer to his prayer – for Beethoven's agony produced beauty; and after the despair came the joy – the exuberant dance movement that follows. Agony and ectasy integrated – a balance given to the universe, through music.

But music seems to be a parable of life – not just because it can express the depths of human emotion or insight, but in its very make-up. A note which gives a good tone is a complex of many 'over-tones' – no note with any richness to it is pure or simple. A harmony is created out of a series of contrasting notes, and often the intensity of the music depends on dissonances being resolved into more perfect intervals. A tune depends on movement in time; it cannot be eternally static, it must move and change. A single note, or combination of notes unchanging, produces an air-raid siren, not music. Only a sequence of different notes can produce melody. Most melodies also require rhythm – a measure of time and movement which gives dynamic and life to the tune.

Is life not something like this? Nothing stands still – but then stagnation is boring. Life means movement and fun, constant questing, making discoveries, developing, being creative. This is the kind of living which is celebration, a kind of beautiful music, an entering into the creative purposes of God. The charlady's idea of heaven, staying in bed all day with endless cups of tea supplied, is not really very attractive. God's new creation must be more like the positive aspects of this life than has traditionally been supposed. This would seem to be expressed in the pictures of a new heaven and a new earth which are painted in the Bible. Richness and complexity are required, as well as movement, to produce music worth playing and life worth living.

There is another way in which music is parabolic. It is firmly earthed in the physical reality of our existence: cat-gut, air in tubes, sound-waves, receivers, ears. Without these concrete things, there is no music. Nor is there music without physical discipline and energetic commitment on the part of the performer – the co-ordination of muscles, the acquisition of skills by practice, training the human body to perform precise tasks. Yet who would claim that that account of music is complete? What about the expressive qualities we first observed, its power to communicate, its spiritual dimension? Music in itself transcends its physical reality, though it is impossible without it. And life is like that too; we know no other existence than an embodied one, a physical existence in a physical environment. Our embodied state is essential for our self-expression, for communication, for creative action, for living and having fun. Yet our natural physical existence does not tell the whole story about us as people in relationship to each other and to God. There is a transcendent or spiritual dimension to ourselves and our experience. At the same time, it is only when the transcendent finds physical expression that it is earthed in reality: there is something wrong with a marriage when physical intimacy goes. There is something wrong with a spirituality which is only 'otherworldly'.

What about the dissonances which give spice and intensity to the music? Is that not also potentially parabolic? What seems good and what seems evil is all intertwined, clashing and resolving, but together weaving a total pattern of beauty, a tapestry of sound which pleases even when it is harsh to the ear. Cross and resurrection cannot be pulled apart. This is not to deny the reality of sin and evil and suffering – the clashes are real enough and solid enough. Yet God is constantly at work re-moulding, sharing and bearing the darkness, so that it is seen in the context of a deeper perspective – his overflowing love. The dissonances contribute to the harmony.

Mozart was the composer who intrigued Karl Barth, and it is significant that he includes one of his musical reflections in the chapter in the *Church Dogmatics* on 'nothingness'. For Barth, nothingness summed up everything opposed to God, everything resistant to his will. Creation is not to be identified with the nothingness, but it is continually confronted with this menace, and clearly has a negative as well as a positive side.

It is true that in creation there is not only a Yes but also a No; not only a height but also an abyss; not only clarity but also obscurity; not only progress and continuation but also impediment and limitation; not only growth but also decay; not only opulence but also indigence; not only beauty but also ashes; not only beginning but also end; not only value but also worthlessness. It is true that in creaturely existence, and especially in the existence of man, there are hours, days and years both bright and dark, success and failure, laughter and tears, youth and age, gain and loss, birth and sooner or later its inevitable corollary, death.

Barth here sums up some of those aspects of the universe which cry out for integration, and whose integration we have been exploring in our study of atonement. Barth, however, insists that the creation is nevertheless good, and he speaks of the creation praising its Creator and Lord even on its shadowy side, even in the negative aspect in which it is so near to nothingness. Then comes his digression on Mozart:

I must again revert to Wolfgang Amadeus Mozart. Why is it that this man is so incomparable? Why is it that for the receptive, he has produced in almost every bar he conceived and composed a type of music for which 'beautiful' is not a fitting epithet: music which for the true Christian is not mere entertainment, enjoyment or edification but food and drink; music full of comfort and counsel for his needs; music which is never a slave to its technique nor sentimental but always 'moving', free and liberating because wise, strong and sovereign? Why is it possible to hold that Mozart has a place in theology . . .

88

although he . . . does not seem to have been a particularly active Christian . . . apparently leading what might appear to us a rather frivolous existence when not occupied with his work? It is possible to give him this position because he knew something about creation in its total goodness that . . . (no theologian) either knows or can express and maintain as he did . . . 1756–1791! This was the time when God was under attack for the Lisbon earthquake, and theologians and other well-meaning folk were hard put to it to defend Him. In the face of the problem of theodicy, Mozart had the peace of God which far transcends all the critical or speculative reason that praises or reproves . . . He had heard, and causes those who have ears to hear, even today, what we shall not see until the end of time – the whole context of providence. As though in the light of this end, he heard the harmony of creation to which the shadow also belongs but in which the shadow is not darkness, deficiency is not defeat, sadness cannot become despair, trouble cannot degenerate into tragedy and infinite melancholy is not ultimately forced to claim undisputed sway. Thus the cheerfulness in this harmony is not without its limits. But the light shines all the more brightly because it breaks forth from the shadow. The sweetness is also bitter and cannot therefore cloy. Life does not fear death but knows it well . . . (Mozart) simply offered himself as the agent by which little bits of horn, metal and catgut could serve as the voices of creation, sometimes leading, sometimes accompanying and sometimes in harmony . . . He himself was only an ear for this music, and its mediator to other ears. He died when according to the worldly wise his life-work was only ripening to its true fulfilment. But who shall say that after the 'Magic Flute', the Clarinet Concerto of October 1791 and the Requiem, it was not already fulfilled? . . .

I make this interposition here, before turning to chaos, be-cause in the music of Mozart . . . we have clear and convincing proof that it is slander on creation to charge it with a share in chaos because it includes a Yes and a No, as though orientated to God on the one side and nothingness on the other. Mozart causes us to hear that even on the latter side, and therefore in its totality, creation praises its Master and is therefore perfect . . . Mozart has created order for those who have ears to hear, and he has done it better than any scientific deduction could.[3]

For Barth, Mozart was so significant because his music could prove that there was no ultimate dualism, and that all things may be so integrated in the presence of God that only praise can be heard. Through Mozart we can discern that the dissonances contribute to the harmony.

It was of course Pythagoras who suggested that music was the clue to the constitution of the universe. Some of what he discovered was right: harmonic intervals do depend on mathematical proportions, and mathematics is essential to understanding the basis of physical reality. More imaginative was his talk of the music of the spheres, but it was not for nothing that the Greek Fathers adopted from Greek literature the picture of God as a lyre-player. God as improvising and adapting, developing, harmonizing, enjoying the music he plays, that is a fascinating thought. Perhaps it is this kind of creative integration of dissonance and harmony which gives us the most telling way of understanding God's atoning activity. Taking up the demonic into art is a way of giving a balance to the universe.

Maybe the objection will be raised that all this is very far from scriptural. Music is not found among Jesus' parables, and the kind of parabolic use made of it here derives from Greek philosophy, not the biblical tradition. That is true. But if God is creator of all, can we not borrow insights from other cultures? In fact, the biblical writers were doing so all the time! Besides, music is at the heart of any celebration. If I am right in stressing the celebratory aspect of sacrifice and worship, the enjoyment and feasting in the kingdom, then music must have its part to play. And of course it does, even in the Bible. The psalms resound with it; C. S. Lewis noticed their gusto, their cheerful spontaneity, their almost physical desire for praising God – their fingers itch for the harp. 'Let's have a song, bring the tambourine, bring the "merry harp with the lute", we're going to sing merrily and make a cheerful noise.'[4] Music and dancing appear in many descriptions of festive occasions in the Old Testament, and are implied in appropriate contexts in the New: look at the parable of the Prodigal Son (Luke 15.25). As for singing, it is encouraged all over the place, for singing is the appropriate vehicle for praising the Lord; the apostles, like the prophets and psalmists before them, sing or encourage others to sing:

> Let the word of Christ dwell in you richly, as you teach and admonish one another in all wisdom, and as you sing psalms and hymns and spiritual songs with thankfulness in your hearts to God (Col. 3.16).

> Be filled with the Spirit, addressing one another in psalms and hymns and spiritual songs, singing and making melody to the Lord with all your heart, always and for everything giving thanks in the name of our Lord Jesus Christ to God the Father (Eph. 5.18b–20).

The bridegroom is present at the wedding-feast, and celebration is appropriate. Music helps the celebration; and by its very nature symbolizes the atoning integration of all things in God. Diversity is necessary, movement is necessary, tension is necessary, to achieve the harmony required. So in the presence of God, let us join in the symphony of all creation.

> Heaven and earth must pass away,
> Songs of praise shall crown that day;
> God will make new heavens, new earth,
> Songs of praise shall hail their birth.

> And will man alone be dumb
> Till that glorious kingdom come?
> No! The Church delights to raise
> Psalms and hymns and songs of praise.

> Saints below, with heart and voice,
> Still in songs of praise rejoice,
> Learning here, by faith and love,
> Songs of praise to sing above.

Borne upon their latest breath,
Songs of praise shall conquer death;
Then amidst eternal joy,
Songs of praise their powers employ.

5

New Birth

After the interlude, back to the business of the evening! We turn now to what has been described as the underlying concern of the whole book – the question how we appropriate our heritage, how we bring alive what we have received from the past. After all, what is it that makes the church different from a social work agency or a political party? It is surely its theology, its scriptures, its words of life – in fact, its heritage. Man does not live by bread alone, and it is only when the treasures of the faith are being appropriated, when atonement is being realized in the life of the church and of Christian individuals, when the gospel is preached and God is worshipped, that the church is being itself.

Creative use of a past heritage cannot simply mean taking it over with no questions asked. Nor can it mean abandoning it as irrelevant. There is continuity and discontinuity, criticism and respect, acceptance and rejection, agreement and disagreement – for dialogue, interplay between past and present is inevitably involved. The New Testament itself provides us with a model of what it means to appropriate the past in a creative way; for those who shaped the thinking of the New Testament were incredibly bold in shifting the application of their scriptures. No longer were the sons of Abraham those descended from him – they were those who responded in faith to God. No longer did Moses reveal all there was to know of God's salvation and God's will; Christ had fulfilled it all and thrown an entirely new light on its true meaning. Earlier we noticed how this happened in the Epistle to the Hebrews: all the mass of legal prescriptions concerning sacrifice were both fulfilled and abrogated because the death of Christ indicated their true meaning; yet they themselves lent meaning to the death of Christ. There was a two-way process, a reciprocal effect: without scripture, God's present activity would not have been recognized, yet that new activity transformed the meaning discerned in the text. Undoubtedly this was true for Paul also. The idea that Christ was simply the end of the law in the sense that the law was finished, over and done with, is a serious misunderstanding of Paul. The law meant *torah*, the five books of teaching which included the story of redemption and revelation. Paul constantly appeals to these books as scripture to back up his arguments. What he meant to convey is that Christ is the clue to the true meaning of the law. The new covenant is written not on stone tablets but on human hearts; yet Paul understood what the covenant meant and what Christ meant through creative meditation on the scriptures. Without *torah* he would never have grasped Christ's significance: yet Christ radically transformed his understanding of *torah*. So for Paul, it is the Christians who are heirs in Christ, those who inherit the promises, those who really perceive the meaning of the scriptures.

Some might wish to argue that this process of reinterpretation was essential then but not now, because then the unique Christ-event had just occurred and, inspired by the Spirit, the apostles were proclaiming this new revelation to the world. Such a cataclysmic event has not happened to force us into new thinking. Up to a point that is a fair enough reaction. Yet it is no good preaching Paul's sermons unchanged to the Cherokee: without translation and reapplication there will be no communication. Nor is it any good preaching the Anselmian theory in Anselm's terms if it has ceased to carry conviction. Reapplication is necessary because the world does not stand still. The concerns, the perceptions, the problems of each generation are different from those of past generations whether subtly or markedly, and we have become increasingly aware of this in this century. Earlier generations failed to perceive the changes, they were so subtle: Augustine belonged to a world he felt to be continuous with that of Plato nearly a thousand years before; the great preacher of the ancient world, John Chrysostom, could believe that when he preached, he adopted unchanged the message – indeed, the *persona* of Paul,[1] even though we can now discern a very considerable shift in outlook. For the need for constant reapplication was always there, and it was done quite unconsciously. This is true not only within the history of the church; modern scholarship has become increasingly interested in the process of redaction within the Bible itself, the way traditions were reinterpreted and reapplied in transmission, both oral and written. The process of making the past come alive is not a new one, nor was it confined to the first generation of Christian believers attempting to assimilate new event and old tradition. Consciously or unconsciously, it has always happened, and must continue to do so. If we are to be heirs in Christ, we need to take seriously both the New Testament's devotion to the scriptures and its freedom in using them, its ability to allow the present and the past to interpret each other. Scripture has to be freed from the kind of love which would fix its language and ossify its meaning for all time, demanding that we can only respond if we force ourselves into the moulds of the past age. Yet scripture must be allowed to speak, to question and challenge us, to contribute to our thinking, to stretch our minds beyond our immediate preoccupations. Creative use of scripture demands this process of dialogue. Both respect and criticism must characterize our approach to the text, and out of the listening and the questioning may come insights which to our surprise meet our needs.

Our study of atonement has been, I hope, a demonstration of the kind of thing possible. We embarked upon that study because questions about its meaning posed themselves with urgent insistence. It should have been clear that these questions were by no means merely academic. To be able to continue living in faith made an answer vitally necessary. We found our way to some kind of answer by looking at past answers, reviewing their strengths and weaknesses, listening with respect to positive contributions, acknowledging their deep influence, but not being afraid to reject and question aspects of the material which did not ring true for us. We sought a resolution of difficulties with the traditional theories by going back to the Bible and taking very seriously two 'dead' ideas: apocalyptic and sacrifice. We found our way to some new insight by grappling with this alien material, trying to do justice to its importance in scripture, deliberately seeking to understand the unfamiliar but thereby discovering that our own perceptions were enriched. And this enrichment did not occur because we tried to transfer out-dated language into the modern world directly; it happened because we found points where insights 'chimed' and led the way to further developments and reflection. Our exploration is unlikely to have solved all the problems, but at least some attempt has been made to engage in creative dialogue with the past and find a way of appropriating our heritage.

Now exactly how does this creative assimilation of scripture take place? Does one begin with the Bible or with modern experience? It seems to me that that very question is misguided. One has to live concurrently committed to both, with both balls in the air, often with the balls entirely out of contact for long periods. The questions posed by life and experience have to be teased at, struggled with, never suppressed. Critical study of the Bible, reflective reading of scripture, wrestling with its meaning, becoming acquainted with its content, all this has to become an on-going habit which does not necessarily pay off immediate dividends but may often seem irrelevant, pursued only for its own sake. It is only if both these things are happening that the creative leaps and associations are possible at moments of disclosure.

If you discuss with a research scientist how he makes his discoveries, he will tell you that the really creative moves occur when he suddenly sees one problem in terms of another, when two apparently unrelated phenomena appear similar in some respect, so that one theory or calculation can be utilized for both situations, perhaps with a little judicious adaptation. There is a fascinating work by Arthur Koestler called *The Act of Creation* in which he sees all creative activities, artistic originality, scientific discovery and even the good joke, as having a basic pattern in common which he calls 'bisociative thinking'. He describes and analyses in his book 'the spontaneous flash of insight which shows a familiar situation or event in a new light'.

> Pythagoras, according to tradition, is supposed to have discovered that musical pitch depends on the ratio between the length of vibrating chords – the starting-point of mathematical physics – by passing in front of the local blacksmith on his native island of Samos, and noticing that rods of iron of different lengths gave different sounds under the blacksmith's hammer. Instead of ascribing it to chance, one suspects that it was obscure intuition which made Pythagoras stop at the blacksmith's shop.[2]

Koestler was searching for how that kind of intuition works. He had discerned that the essence of discovery lay in 'the unlikely marriage of cabbages and kings – of previously unrelated frames of reference or universes of discourse – whose union will solve the previously insoluble problem'. He further noted that 'the search for the improbable partner usually involves long and arduous striving'; but he came to the conclusion that the ultimate matchmaker is the unconscious which generates improbable analogies through the dream and half-dream. In his chapter on 'Moments of Truth', Koestler cites many examples of scientists confessing that the solution to their problem came in a flash, when they were just waking or doing something quite unrelated to the problem. Often it came utterly unexpectedly when the problem was blocked and appeared insoluble. For instance, Henri Poincaré: 'I went to spend a few days at the seaside, and thought of something else. One morning, walking on the bluff, the idea came to me . . .'. And Jacques Hadamard: 'On being very abruptly awakened by an external noise, a solution long searched for appeared to me at once without the slightest instant of reflection on my part . . . and in a quite different direction from any of those which I had previously tried to follow.' And

Karl Friedrich Gauss: 'At last two days ago I succeeded, not by
dint of painful effort but so to speak, by the grace of God. As a
sudden flash of light, the enigma was solved . . . For my part
I am unable to name the nature of the thread which connected
what I previously knew with that which made my success
possible.'

Now this is surely somewhat parallel to the inspired relating
of past and present which lies at the root of appropriating the
tradition, the kind of thing we observed happening in the New
Testament. There comes a sudden illumination which prophe-
tically discerns what is going on in the present because of what
has gone on in the past, which sees that the Bible or the tradition
has important and relevant connections with contemporary
experience – though there is not a one-to-one straightforward
correspondence which enables a simple 'literal' lifting from one
context to another. This is to be likened to creative inspiration
in other fields in that it cannot happen by effort and searching,
or by making deliberate and forced correlations. Typology at its
best, I suggest, was the product of creative association, and
ancient typology has its counterpart in the recent use of the
Exodus-motif in liberation-theology. Both have seen one situation in terms of another and powerful new insights have been
the result. But typology became an exegetical trick encouraging
forced allegory, and so it ossified. The creative insight is an
inspiration, not a technique. Yet for that inspiration to occur
conditions have to be right. No connections will be made if we
know little about the two areas which might be fruitfully brought
into association. That is why both balls have to be kept in the
air. Whether it seems relevant or not, study of the Bible and the
tradition must be pursued for its own sake. Questions about our
experience in the modern world, and the relation of faith to that
experience, must be passionately engaged in, even if the problems
seem insoluble. Maybe the balls appear totally disconnected,
juggled independently; but at least if they are in the air there is
the possibility of one hitting the other when the frustration of
having a problem blocked stimulates the unconscious creative
leap. Simone Weil's advocacy of serious disciplined study as a

means of developing the concentration so necessary for proper prayer and proper pastoral work is not, after all, the only justification for taking academic theology or 'pure research' seriously. Any scientist will defend the continuation of apparently irrelevant pure scientific investigation on the grounds that you never know what will be its pay-off. I would defend biblical criticism and theological study on the same grounds. You never know when a creative 'bisociation' will issue from a deep immersion in the Christian heritage undertaken with a proper balance between critical distance and humble respect.

This suggestion is not merely a neat bit of theory; it is something I have experienced myself, at least on a small scale and at a personal level. Indeed, behind the study of atonement made earlier lies an interesting combination of 'pure research' and moments of truth something like what Koestler describes. These moments had the same ingredients of long wrestling with problems at the intellectual and at the emotional level, a desperate sense of the solution being blocked, and then the flash of insight which 'bisociated' my problem with my academic pursuits. To lay bare such moments is to expose oneself, and it is with some embarrassment that I proceed, especially as one's individual concerns seem trivial in relation to the problems of the world. Yet for the sake of clarity, let me give an account of two of the most significant points of discovery which have contributed to the understanding of atonement offered here.

For years I had worked at the interpretation of Paul as an academic exercise, a piece of fascinating historical study to be read about, thought about, lectured on. There came a period in my private life when I was living with certain tensions and frustrations in my domestic situation, containing it all for the most part successfully, until a moment of crisis – something cracked. I wanted to walk out of the house and just go on walking, right out of the situation, to reach freedom. Yet I knew that that was no solution nor was it really what I wanted to do; my emotional reactions arose out of my own lack of loving accommodation, my own resentment at being at the beck and call of other people – what with in-laws and kids in the house.

This knowledge made me hate myself and my inability to be the sort of person I ought to be. In the midst of all the turmoil and distress, it suddenly came to me that this was what Paul was talking about, especially in Romans 7; Paul knew what frustration with oneself was like, and yet he had been given something which enabled him to live with it. That flash produced immediate and miraculous release – indeed, a realization of the gospel within my own experience. It was hardly an original insight, but coming at that moment of crisis gave it power. Neither my understanding of Paul nor my Christian life has remained unaffected by that moment when the two balls actually came into contact. I can appreciate much more keenly the importance of the present tenses in Romans 7: Paul was not talking about pre-conversion and post-conversion states, nor was he simply doing a midrash on Genesis; Paul was wrestling with the eschatological tension of the Christian's existence. He knew that for a time he was still compromised by being involved in the 'present evil age', the corruption of the world and the flesh; yet as far as God was concerned, in relation to the ultimate judgment and the new creation of the future, he had already been freed from his inadequacies, his 'body of death', his sin – so thanks be to God through Jesus Christ our Lord! Maybe we would not put it quite like that, but another way of putting the same thing might be this; in Christ a person may be utterly realistic about himself and yet live with himself. One can dare to look on one's own selfishness and pride, with shame and yet with confidence in God. To realize that brings an inner peace and gratitude which reduces the sense of frustration and transforms one's reactions to others, so that relationships are genuinely changed for the better. Thus in our personal experience we can share to some degree Paul's perspective on a good creation corrupted but in process of rebirth.

My other moment of truth was triggered by an urgent search for a sermon. For years I had wrestled with the problem of evil, of inadequacy, defectiveness, corruption, suffering and death, not merely at the philosophical level but at the personal level, trying to find a way of understanding how the Creator could be loving – or even be at all – when so much disaster seemed to afflict his world in general, and in particular the creation of my own son had gone so badly wrong. I had also been professionally engaged in studying and interpreting John's Gospel, in probing its world of thought, the background to its theology, its purpose and meaning. One year when it was Mental Handicap week, I found myself in the position of having to preach. I felt utterly helpless. Suddenly and quite unexpectedly, John 9 came alive and provided me with a sermon spoken out of the depths of my personal experience of despair and release. That chapter could speak to me not just because it is about a man born with a handicap. After all, the explicit comment made in v.3 is not very promising or helpful; did God really inflict blindness on the man just so that Jesus could show off by performing a miracle? How callous could he get? Rather it was because I suddenly saw it in the light of John's Gospel as a whole, so that all my reflections on Johannine theology were integrated while at the same time suggestive insights were provided which were able to address my personal problem. The Gospel presents us with a drama. The world is in darkness, and into the darkness comes the light. The light confronts the darkness and the darkness cannot comprehend it; it rejects it and tries to put it out: Jesus Christ is crucified. Yet this is not defeat. For the moment when Christ enters the deepest depths of darkness on the cross is seen as the very hour of glory, the moment when the light blazes forth, consumes the darkness and draws all men to itself. So in the mystery of the cross we see God himself taking responsibility for the situation, God himself invading the darkness, suffering the evil, taking it all upon himself and triumphantly conquering it. Now the Gospel does not spell it all out quite as explicitly as that; yet if we see the discussion in John 9.2f. in this perspective, then its thrust is clearer. The healing of the blind man is, as all commentators have seen, a sign of the giving of light to the world, an acted parable of the transformation of darkness into light, an anticipation of the triumph of the cross. But that does not mean that the darkness is dismissed by a miracle, wafted away with a magic wand. Resurrection does not cancel or invalidate the cross. There is no pretence that the darkness does

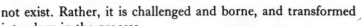

not exist. Rather, it is challenged and borne, and transformed into glory in the process.

Now all that gives no very clear theoretical answer to the problem of evil's existence, and at the level of critical reflection I could not swallow the dualism implied by such an account. Yet in a flash the story came alive for me, and when it did so, with all its implications, it made it possible for me to discern the presence of God in the tragedy of the world, indeed in my own experience of darkness, and seeing the situation in that perspective brought about its own transformation. It seems as if sudden 'chiming' with an old story is often the way the Spirit works. This was the lifeline, and for all its inadequacies it has enabled the subsequent piecing together of the jig-saw, drawing in other apparently unrelated pieces of academic study as well as literature, poetry, music – each pursued for its own sake, each in its own cubby-hole as it were, yet at various moments of disclosure suddenly seen in a new light, fitted together so that thinking and feeling, praying and living were enriched and integrated at new levels. Creative appropriation of our heritage is only possible if both balls are kept in the air, however unpromising and irrelevant the disciplined and critical study of scripture and tradition may sometimes seem.

Given the importance and the possibility of appropriating our heritage, where is it to take place in the life of the church? Well, one hopes that one makes some small contribution by writing books, but surely it must principally go on in preaching. For most church members, academic study can be no more than a dream, and they are bound to receive the tradition 'second-hand'. This does not mean their faith is second-hand, but it does mean that it will be fed and enlarged by others who have the responsibility to carry out that task. The word of preaching cannot help being the main context in which the word of scripture might be expected to come alive for the majority of the faithful. Now preaching is widely regarded as outmoded, as reflecting an authoritarian concept of the church and of the clergy which is not acceptable in the modern world. Discussion, participation – that is what people are after, they say. Should not groups be at work on the job? Well, of course, groups have an important role, but talking-shops with no input soon revolve around in the little circles of the limited experience of the participants. Furthermore, it is in the context of worship, I suggest, that the treasures of Christian experience down the centuries needs to be handed on, to enlarge the vision and deepen the praying of the community. Re-presenting what the past has to tell us in such a way that it comes alive in the present and informs our understanding and our action – that surely is the fundamental task of preaching. Yet at the moment preaching tends to lean over backwards to be relevant and fails to draw on the insights of the tradition, except in a very simple and uncritical way – fails even to communicate the content and thrust of the Bible. So it has mostly become shallow and dull. No wonder it is out of fashion!

Once more the Bible itself provides an effective model of what we should be aiming at. For the book of Deuteronomy appears to be the deposit of a long preaching tradition carried out by Levites. The burden of their message is a reminder that a certain style of life is required by God, coupled with a reworking of what that means now that settled agricultural life has replaced the old nomadic way. The preachers recall their hearers to the 'old-fashioned' virtues of loyalty to God and to each other, respect for God and for each other, even consideration of the outsider; and they do so effectively because they apply these old values to the new social situation, not only in vague general terms, but also in terms of particular laws of property, debt, compensation, precise rules for social behaviour, legal transactions, and religious observances. They have no inhibitions about changing and developing particular laws so as to offer a specific challenge to a particular life-style under God. But this challenge is based on other reminders; remember what God has done – he brought you out of Egypt; remember what God is like – he executes justice for the disadvantaged; remember the privilege of the covenant – he chose you above all peoples. Such reminders form a constant refrain and provide the motivation for a response which is not simply a matter of duty, but arises out of obligation, gratitude, love: 'Circumcize the foreskin of your heart', and recognize that 'God is your praise' (10.16,21).

Stimulating the appropriate response of gratitude, the sense of obligation, requires the two complimentary movements of recalling the past and reminting it so that it comes alive in the present and its practical outworkings become clear. Thus current understanding of how the book of Deuteronomy came to be highlights the task of the preacher. Only by a similar process of focussing attention on the old story of redemption and creatively adapting its message can we appropriate our heritage so that our worship is fertilized and bears fruit. That is the preacher's fundamental responsibility to the church. It is an awesome and demanding role, and it is one that must not be shirked. We desperately need the reminder of God's grace, the assurance of God's presence, the reminting of God's challenge to our mediocrity.

So this is where our two themes come together: for the rebirth of the old-fashioned and outmoded, the Bible, the creeds, the tradition, preaching, involves rediscovering the fact that at the heart of it all is a message about rebirth, a message of hope and atonement, about the possibility of new creation. Of course the birth-pangs go on. The kingdom is coming but is not yet. Nevertheless, in spite of being warped by the imperfections of this world, Chesterfield church spire still points to heaven. We ourselves and the church to which we belong, are warped and inadequate; yet we are the indicators that the atoning process is going on in the world, we are the 'evidence' for resurrection. One way or another it is in the church that people are born again and are adopted as heirs of the kingdom through Christ. It is God who agonizes in bringing the new creation to birth, yet we are called to participate and to bear the agony with joy and hope because he is at work in us and through us.

To bring this to awareness in the life of the church is the task of preaching. What the preacher has to stimulate is precisely the realism and the hope we have seen as the core of the gospel. What the preacher has to offer is the gracious gift of God's atoning presence. What the preacher has to demand is appropriate response, joyful worship offered out of a sense of gratitude and obligation, so that the presence of God is realized in the church and the people are taken up into holy fellowship with him, sanctifying the whole of life to his service. That is effected by communication of the depth and riches of our heritage, and such communication cannot be performed by sitting light to serious study of the roots of our faith. We need to be soaked in the language of scripture and tradition, as were the preachers of the past. Yet we also need the confidence and freedom to rethink and reapply, to see how the old story of atonement is to be reborn in our own time, for the people of our own generation. We need to use the Bible creatively, and to learn that delicate balance between respect and criticism so essential to the appropriation of our heritage.

Epilogue

The Lord said to me, 'Can these dry bones live?' I answered, 'O Lord God, thou knowest.' He said, 'Prophesy to these bones . . . Behold I will cause breath to enter you, and you shall live . . . and you shall know that I am the Lord.' (Ezek. 37.3–6).

Theology, the Bible, preaching – are these today's dry bones? If so, why are they dead? Is it because we just accept them as a matter of habit without attempting to understand or assimilate? Or is it because we are too prone to neglect or discard without proper foresight what seems difficult or alien? What this book has attempted is the exploration of texts and ideas, perspectives and doctrines, that have apparently gone dead, in the hope that by making an effort of investigation and imagination, we may rediscover their potential. Could it be that with the right gift of the Spirit, they might be invested with new life? Could it be that with the right determination to investigate and think and understand, there is a possibility of new birth?

In the Bible, birth and resurrection are intimately related ideas. The doctrine of resurrection parallels the doctrine of creation; for both involve imparting the breath of life. In Genesis 2, God takes the dry dust of the desert, dampens it, shapes the clay and breathes in life. In Ezekiel 37, the prophet sees a vision of Israel restored – dry bones reassembled, covered with flesh, and brought to life by the breath of God's Spirit.

Such images of creation and new life eventually stimulated the idea of resurrection – of the dead restored, of a new creative act of God, new and yet continuous with the old. Birth, too, involves the giving of life, and in Romans 4 subtle play on the association of birth and resurrection lies at the core of Paul's argument. The essence of Abraham's faith was that he put his trust in God's power to produce life in the midst of deadness: not even the thought of his own body, so old it was practically deadened, nor of Sarah's womb, barren, lifeless, dead as it was, could deflect Abraham from his fundamental trust that God could bring life out of death and so fulfil his promise. Likewise, Paul suggests, the essence of Christian faith is trust in the God who has brought life from death in the resurrection of Christ. The parallel is pressed through Paul's choice of words, a fact obscured in nearly every translation, but striking in the original Greek. It is because Abraham's faith and Christian faith share the same quality, have the same basis, focus on the same grasp of God's life-giving power, that Paul can so confidently apply to Christians the statement about Abraham – that his faith was accepted as equivalent to righteousness.

But that liberating parallel could only be pressed because Paul had come to see the Jewish scriptures in a new perspective. A death had to come first. If old ideas are to find new birth, it is likely that something like the same process will have to occur. For birth is a labour which is hard and painful. If renewal is to come, we have to face the pain of lost assumptions and the labour of rethinking. So this book is meant to be a challenge – a challenge to all those who are tempted to retreat from asking questions and plead the sufficiency of a simple traditional faith; to all those who go for 'gut-theology', claiming that their Christian faith is a matter of the heart only, and not the head; to all those who treat ministry as a form of social work or personal counselling rather than communication of the Word of God; to all those who have allowed the Bible to drift to the periphery, perhaps because they feel threatened or incapacitated by critical study rather than liberated and enabled; but no less, to all those who have put the Bible on a pedestal and worshipped it without really investigating its contents. New life poured out in abundance is at the heart of the Christian message; yet a baby yells at the prospect of the unknown future, and growing to maturity involves a painful process of constant rebirth. Can we face it? Not as long as we retreat into a dry defensiveness or an embarrassed reductionism.

Birth and resurrection are intimately related ideas. So the themes of this book revolve around new beginnings on old foundations, new growth grafted on to the old stump, resurrection which is new creation and yet the dead restored; in other words, continuity and discontinuity with tradition. What we have embarked on is a quest for renewed inspiration and energy from the living faith of the past, and for ways of appropriating that faith creatively. This initial expedition is unlikely to have uncovered much of the hidden treasure that we seek; yet the very quest for a creative way of putting God and the Bible back at the centre must surely be worthwhile; and it could be an enterprise with enormous potential for the future of ecumenism and the renewal of the church. But it will demand of the church at every level the Lenten discipline of paying attention to the Word of God, of refusing to be satisfied with naïve or dogmatic answers, or with any superficiality in the basic work of reading, thinking and praying. It will demand the discipline of daring to abandon a tame traditionalism, and yet taking tradition very seriously. In Hans von Balthasar's words:

> To be faithful to the tradition is not after all to repeat and transmit literally certain philosophical and theological statements which one imagines transcend time and the contingencies of history. Rather it is to copy from our Fathers in the faith the attitude of intense reflection and the effort of bold creation, necessary preludes for true spiritual faithfulness.

Such an undertaking is only possible if we are prepared to cut loose the moorings and set out trusting as Paul and Abraham did in a God who is able to bring life out of death.

The Lord said to me, 'Can these dry bones live?' I answered, 'O Lord God, thou knowest.' He said, 'Prophesy to these bones . . . Behold, I will cause breath to enter you, and you shall live . . . and you shall know that I am the Lord.'

NOTES

1 As Little Children

1. *Children's Letters to God,* compiled by Eric Marshall and Stuart Hample, Fontana 1976. (A 1991 new American edition, *Children's Letters to God: The New Collection,* was published by Workman Publishing Co.)

2. From an unpublished essay by Ken Witts, now retired to Gobowen.

3. From a letter written by Alfred Williams to a friend, quoted in Leonard Clark, *Alfred Williams. His Life and Work,* David and Charles 1969, pp. 18–19. (A 1969 American edition was published by Kelley.)

4. The complete essay can be found in *Waiting on God,* Routledge 1951; Fontana 1959, pp. 66–76. (A 1981 American edition was published by Whitaker House.)

5. Fynn, *Mister God, This is Anna,* Collins 1974; Fount 1977, pp. 28ff., 39ff. (A 1985 American edition was published by Ballantine.)

2 The Outstretched Arms

1. Heinemann 1935; Corgi 1958, p. 68.

2. OUP 1966, pp. 254–5.

3. Paul Tillich, *Systematic Theology,* Vol 2, University of Chicago Press and James Nisbet 1957; SCM Press 1978, pp. 172f.

4. F. R. Barry, *The Atonement,* Hodder 1968, p. 140.

5. Leon Morris, *The Apostolic Preaching of the Cross,* Tyndale Press 1955.

6. Peter Abelard, *Commentary on Romans* II (on 3.26), ed. E. M. Buytaert, *Corpus Christianorum,* Continuatio Mediaevalis xi, p. 118 (my translation).

7. Ibid., p. 117.
8. Abelard and Héloise, Letter 4, trans. by Betty Radice, The Folio Society 1977, pp. 92–5.
9. Tillich, op. cit., p. 172.
10. A selection of significant works is as follows. On the Anselmian side: R. W. Dale, *The Atonement* (1875); J. Denney, *The Death of Christ* (1903) and *The Christian Doctrine of Reconciliation* (1917); and J. Rivière, *The Doctrine of Atonement* (ET 1909)—a Catholic history. On the liberal side: R. C. Moberly, *Atonement and Personality* (1901); R. S. Franks, *A History of the Doctrine of the Work of Christ* (1918); H. Rashdall, *The Idea of Atonement in Christian Theology* (1919). (A 1981 American edition of *The Death of Christ* was published as part of the Shephard Illustrated Classic Series by Keats. A 1918[?] American edition of *The Christian Doctrine of Reconciliation* was published by the George H. Doran Company.)
11. Gustaf Aulen, *Christus Victor*, SPCK 1931. (A 1992 American edition was published by Peter Smith.)
12. The works referred to are: H. A. Hodges, *The Pattern of Atonement*, SCM Press 1955, and *Death and Life Have Contended*, SCM Press 1964; F. R. Barry, *The Atonement* (see n. 4 above); F. W. Dillistone, *The Christian Understanding of Atonement*, James Nisbet 1968; and R. Leivestad, *Christ the Conqueror. Ideas of Conflict and Victory in the New Testament*, SPCK 1954. (A 1968[?] American edition of *The Christian Understanding of Atonement* was published by Westminster Press.)
13. Frances M. Young, *Sacrifice and Death of Christ*, SPCK 1975. (A 1978[?] American edition was published by Westminster Press.)
14. Chaim Potok, *My Name is Asher Lev*, Heinemann 1972, pp. 329f. (A 1984 American edition was published by Fawcett.)

3 The Woman in Travail

1. For some discussion and bibliography, see the review articles on the prophetic literature and the Psalms by W. McKane and J. H. Eaton in *Tradition and Interpretation*, ed. G. W. Anderson, OUP 1979; also J. H. Eaton, *Festal-drama in Deutero-Isaiah*, SPCK 1979, and *Vision in Worship*, SPCK 1981.

2. John Day, 'A Case of Inner Scriptural Interpretation', *JTS* NS 31, 1980, pp. 309–19.

3. See C. Westermann, *Isaiah* 40–66, SCM Press 1969, pp. 105–6. (A 1969 American edition was published as part of the Old Testament Library by Westminster.)

4. *Hymns of Thanksgiving* (III.7–10), translation by Millar Burrows in his *The Dead Sea Scrolls*, Secker & Warburg 1956, p. 403. (A 1955 American edition was published by Viking Press.)

5. Notably by Jürgen Moltmann in *Theology of Hope*, SCM Press 1967; see further the comments of Sophie Laws, 'Can Apocalyptic be relevant?' in *What about The New Testament?*, Essays in honour of Christopher Evans, ed. Morna Hooker and Colin Hickling, SCM Press 1975, pp. 89–102. (A 1967 American edition of *Theology of Hope* was published by Harper and Row.)

6. Chaim Potok, *My Name is Asher Lev*, pp. 367f.

7. From 'Selected Pensées of Simone Weil' to be found in *Gateway to God*, ed. David Raper, Fontana 1974, pp. 48, 54, 55. These Pensées have been taken from her published work as follows: *First and Last Notebooks*, OUP 1970, pp. 103, 120; *Intimations of Christianity*, Routledge 1957, pp. 193f.; *Notebooks* Vol II, Routledge 1956, p. 424.

8. From 'Some reflections on the Love of God', *Gateway to God*, pp. 80f.; taken from *On Science, Necessity and the Love of God*, OUP 1968.

9. Tillich, *Systematic Theology*, Vol 2, pp. 174ff.

10. *Dying We Live*, ed. Helmut Gollwitzer, Käthe Kuhn, and Reinhold Schneider, Fontana 1958. The following quotations will be found on pp. 25, 36, 97f., 80f. (A 1956[?] American edition was published by Pantheon.)

11. Rudolf Otto, *The Idea of the Holy*, OUP 1923; Penguin 1959, pp. 60–72.

12. See my discussions of this question in *The Myth of God Incarnate*, ed. John Hick, SCM Press 1977, and *Incarnation and Myth*, ed. Michael Goulder, SCM Press 1979. (A 1977 American edition of *The Myth of God* was published by Westminster Press. A 1967 American edition of *Incarnation and Myth* was published by Books on Demand.)

4   The Wedding Feast

1. Originally one of the Moffatt New Testament Commentaries, Hodder 1932; Fontana 1959.

2. Originally published as 'ILASKESTHAI in The Septuagint', *JTS* 32, 1931, pp. 352–60; republished in *The Bible and the Greeks*, Hodder 1935.

3. See ch. 2, n. 5.

4. For a fuller discussion of all this, see my *Sacrifice and the Death of Christ*. The extra-biblical material in the following discussion is drawn from my earlier work.

5. Quotations from G. Vermes, *The Dead Sea Scrolls in English*, Penguin 1962, pp. 87–90.

6. For the various points made see: *De Spec. Leg.* I.257, 167, etc.; *Sac*, 84; *Plant.* 108, 126; *Deus* 7–8; *Det.* 20–21.

7. C. G. Montefiore and H. Loewe, *A Rabbinic Anthology*, Macmillan 1938, pp. 430–1.

8. *De Civitate Dei* x.6.

A Musical Interlude

1. From a record sleeve; Vox Productions Inc., USA.

2. *God of a Hundred Names*, Prayers of many peoples and creeds collected and arranged by Barbara Greene and Victor Gollancz, Gollancz 1962; Hodder 1975, p. 207. (A 1963 American edition was published by Doubleday.)

3. Karl Barth, *Church Dogmatics* III.3.50, T. & T. Clark 1961, pp. 296f., 297ff. I am grateful to Dr David Ford for drawing my attention to this passage.

4. C. S. Lewis, *Reflections on the Psalms*, Geoffrey Bles 1958; Fontana 1961, pp. 47–8. (A 1958 American edition was published by Harcourt Brace.)

5   New Birth

1. I am indebted to Alan Morrison, a graduate student at Birmingham University, for illuminating comments on this point.

2. Arthur Koestler, *The Act of Creation,* Hutchinson 1964, 1969; Pan Books 1970, pp. 111f. (A 1964 American edition was published by Macmillan.)

INDEX

Index

Self-sufficiency, 27, 79–80
Seminarians. *See* Ordinands
Septuagint, 66–68
Sermon on the Mount, 10
Sin, 22, 23, 26–27, 36–37, 56, 58–59, 66–73, 79, 100
Spirituality, 41, 87
Steinbeck, John, 21, 40
Structuralism, 14
Suffering, 16–17, 22, 58

Supernaturalism, 10, 12

Theodicy, 57, 89
Typology, 98

Weil, Simone, 15, 57–58, 98
Woman in travail, ix, 43–50, 58, 62. *See also* Birth
Worship, 72–74, 78–83, 93, 103–5